MARRIAGE ON TRIAL

THE CASE AGAINST

SAME-SEX MARRIAGE

AND PARENTING

GLENN T. STANTON
AND DR. BILL MAIER

InterVarsity Press
Downers Grove, Illinois

InterVarsity Press
P.O. Box 1400, Downers Grove, IL 60515-1426
World Wide Web: www.ivpress.com
E-mail: mail@ivpress.com

InterVarsity Press® is the book-publishing division of InterVarsity Christian Fellowship/USA®, a student movement active on campus at hundreds of universities, colleges and schools of nursing in the United States of America, and a member movement of the International Fellowship of Evangelical Students. For information about local and regional activities, write Public Relations Dept., InterVarsity Christian Fellowship/USA, 6400 Schroeder Rd., P.O. Box 7895, Madison, WI 53707-7895, or visit the IVCF website at <www.intervarsity.org>.

Design: Cindy Kiple

Images: Hisham F. Ibrahim/Getty Images

ISBN 0-8308-3274-2

Printed in the United States of America ∞

Library of Congress Cataloging-in-Publication Data

Stanton, Glenn T., 1962-
   Marriage on trial: the case against same-sex marriage and
parenting / Glenn T. Stanton, Bill Maier.
    p. cm.
   Includes bibliographical references.
   ISBN 0-8308-3274-2 (pbk.: alk. paper)
   1. Same-sex marriage. 2. Gay parents. 3. Marriage—Religious
aspects—Christianity. 4. Family—Religious aspects—Christianity.
   I. Maier, Bill II. Title.
   HQ1033.S726 2004
   306.84'8—dc22

                                                     2004011522

P	19	18	17	16	15	14	13	12	11	10	9	8	7	6	5	4	3	2	1
Y	19	18	17	16	15	14	13	12	11	10	09	08	07	06	05	04			

To our children, their generation and their children after them.

"The trick is, gay leaders and pundits must stop watering the issue down—'this is simply about equality for gay couples'—and offer same-sex marriage for what it is: an opportunity to reconstruct a traditionally homophobic institution by bringing it to our more equitable queer value system."

OUT, May 1996

"Let times change, let the weather change, but do not invent an adulterated family and drink from it as if it were the real nourishing thing."

Alvaro de Silva, *Brave New Family*

CONTENTS

NOTE TO READERS

We have designed *Marriage on Trial* as an "equipping manual" that will prepare you to make a reasoned, persuasive case when defending natural marriage and responding to same-sex marriage arguments. It will also provide you with accurate information on the nature of homosexuality and the conflicting positions regarding same-sex marriage *within* the gay community. To that end, this book is written in a "question and answer" format, allowing you to find the answers you are seeking more easily.

In order for each answer to stand on its own and give you what you need in one place, we have repeated some research in different places in the book. We have only done this where such research is foundational to the questions asked and its reiteration useful. We pray that you will find this book helpful as you contend for the natural family with friends, relatives and coworkers.

Glenn T. Stanton
William J. Maier

Acknowledgments

Our thanks go to many individuals for their indispensable input and encouragement: Dean Byrd at the University of Utah, Warren Throckmorton at Grove City College, Mark Yarhouse at Regent University, Stan Jones at Wheaton College, and Joe and Linda Nicolosi at the National Association for the Research and Therapy of Homosexuality (NARTH). Pete Winn, our colleague, contributed to our thinking in some of the early questions. Virginia Wing, Glenn's summer intern, assembled the very helpful and comprehensive index. Dr. Gary Deddo, our editor at InterVarsity Press, recognized the importance of this project and served as a wise guide and helpful encourager, keeping us prepared and online for every deadline.

Special thanks go to Dr. James Dobson who has given us the encouragement and opportunity to study, think and teach others on critical family issues. Our culture is indebted to his inspirational leadership in protecting and strengthening the family.

Finally, to our precious and patient wives who tolerated our distracted hours and days of research, speaking trips and writing. Jacqueline (Glenn) and Lisa (Bill), you help us make sense of life, giving it fullness, perspective, meaning and the sweet mystery of otherness. You are gifts and we honor you!

How This Book Will Equip You to Make the Case for Marriage

Same-sex marriage. Same-sex parenting. Can we make the gay family just as socially necessary and normal as the natural family?

Does it really matter if we define marriage and the family one way as opposed to another? Can't families be anything we want them to be? Are men and women optional for marriage or are mothers and fathers interchangeable in the family? Are there good reasons for saying marriage should be for life, bringing men and women together to build a cooperative life and create and raise the next generation of humanity? In these pages we explore these questions and discover *why* marriage can't be anything we want it to be. To do so is to radically redefine a fundamental and historic human institution. *To do so is to deconstruct humanity.*

In this book we think about why marriage and parenting are something done between a man and a woman, and why it is hurtful to do it any other way.

Before we address the question of same-sex marriage and parenting, we need to understand the case offered by same-sex marriage proponents. It's pretty straightforward. For most advocates the issue is about fairness and access to certain legal and financial benefits. As we will see later, for some it is about deconstructing or redefining the family.

The first group queries, "If heterosexuals can fall in love and form committed relationships called marriage, why can't homosexuals?" Likewise, they protest, "If heterosexuals gain access to legal, tax and health benefits with their marriages, why can't homosexuals have access to these same benefits when they commit themselves to another?" Their case for same-sex parenting is that kids need loving parents, and two men or two women can love and care for a child as well as a mother and a father can. Some even contend they can do it better.

But we must be honest here. These arguments serve the interest of those making the argument. They are not at all about serving the common good. But marriage is never only about the couple. It is always about the larger community. Marriage is an agreement between a couple *and* the larger society. Concern for the good of all society is the only reason social institutions such as churches and government get involved at all. Marriage is not just for the benefit of the couple. In fact it always includes concern about the next generation as well. We seem to have forgotten this.

As we shall discover in this book, every society needs marriage to

- regulate sexuality, keeping it confined to committed, loving, exclusive relationships

- socialize men, channeling their sexual and masculine energy in community-building ways

- protect women from being exploited by men

- ensure that children grow up with biologically connected mothers and fathers

Marriage serves these purposes in all known human civilizations, and it does so because it brings men and women together in permanent, exclusive relationships. Same-sex marriage is incapable of doing any of these things. There is simply no social need for "same-sex marriage." But all societies *need* natural marriage.[1]

Ask yourself, "Could society be harmed by too much same-sex marriage?" The answer, which we will document, is yes. Then ask this question, "Is too much natural (heterosexual) marriage ever harmful to society?" Such marriages pose no danger—no danger—no matter how pervasive. Rather, it may be the fact that too *little* of it would be harmful. Therefore, same-sex and

---

[1]"Natural marriage" is a phrase we use to refer to marriage as it has always existed in all human civilizations: a socially recognized and encouraged institution which uniquely brings the two parts of humanity—male and female—together in a cooperative, complementary sexual and domestic relationship. We recognize that men and women do marriage differently in different cultures, but marriage arises in all cultures as a way to bring men and women together exclusively in domestic life.

natural marriage cannot be regarded as equal in social value and benefit. Society needs one but has no vital need of the other.

This book, then, is centered around two fundamental questions:

1. *What is the purpose of marriage?*

2. *Are a male and a female parent necessary for children?*

These questions form the center of the debate. There can be no getting around it if we're concerned not just about married couples but about the welfare of our present and future society.

IS THIS BOOK FOR YOU?

"Surely gays have the same right to marry that heterosexuals do?"

"Isn't banning gays from marriage just like banning interracial marriage?"

"How does someone's gay marriage threaten your family?"

"It doesn't matter for children as long as they have two loving parents."

"But lots of other cultures have different ways of forming families. Why can't we?"

We all have heard these questions and concerns offered as "reasons" for why same-sex marriage should be allowed in our society. Do they point us to the truth, or are there good answers in response? How do we respond?

This book shows you that there are very compelling, caring and commonsense ways to answer *every* argument you might encounter in this debate. It will arm you with cogent and loving answers so that you can be an intelligent and compassionate advocate for marriage.

This book is written for people who care about marriage and care about people. It is written in a conversational way to help you easily answer questions about this issue that are swirling all around us in the public debate. It is written in very plain language and is well-documented by the latest research.

We will equip you to understand and explain (1) how harmful same-sex marriage and parenting can be to people and our culture, and (2) why natural marriage between one man and one woman is so important to the health of humanity.

How This Book Is Organized

In the first section of this book we examine and answer the most popular claims of same-sex proponents. But it is not enough to merely understand why same-sex unions are not a good idea. We have to also understand why marriage, as it has existed through all of history, is deeply beneficial to humans. That is why, in the second section, we explore what marriage is; how it benefits adults, children and society; and why the gender difference inherent in marriage is essential to its success in bringing good things to our lives. In the final section, we explore the nature of homosexuality itself and ask some very important questions: Is it rooted in nature? Can homosexuals change? Is it good for people? and Do same-sex marriage advocates really care about marriage?

These three sections will help you understand what supporters of same-sex marriage claim, think about why those claims are wrong, and explain to friends and family why marriage between persons of opposite gender—as imperfect as it sometimes can be—benefits children and our society.

Is Opposition to Same-Sex Marriage and Parenting Rooted in Bigotry?

But before we begin to discuss the issue at hand, it is important to understand and clarify what this issue *is* and *is not* about.

This debate over same-sex marriage is *not* a discussion of

- whether homosexuals are nice people or good citizens. Some are; some are not, just like heterosexuals.
- whether homosexuals can form caring relationships. Of course they can.
- whether homosexuals can be loving parents. Few would deny this.
- whether homosexuals should be treated with dignity. Of course, every member of the human race should be treated with dignity. (We must remember that each of us is a prodigal son or daughter who needs forgiveness from the unbounded grace of the Father.)

In the midst of this debate we need to confront the accusation that if someone is against same-sex marriage then they are automatically homophobic and mean-spirited. When we debate this issue publicly, we have some opponents who accuse us of these flaws—even before there is any discussion. This prejudgment tends to shut down all civil debate before it gets started. Other opponents, though, stick to the issues and engage us very civilly. It is our hope that all parties in this debate would respect one another as fellow humans and debate the issues without being accusatory and prejudicial. And both sides can be guilty of this: charges of homophobia on one side and sexual libertinism on the other are not helpful.

We must ask, Is it possible to oppose homosexuality and still love people who are homosexuals? As Christians we are commanded to do both. But unfortunately some of the pro-gay rhetoric has made it seem nearly impossible for anyone to answer yes to this question. However, this is very unhelpful. It shuts down civil debate. *It is important for each of us to understand how this shift in rhetoric has happened, and how it was deliberately made to make any moral criticism, even that given out of concern for the good of individuals or society, seem unloving or cruel.* Writer and social critic Mark Steyn notes how simple it was for this shift to take place, rooted as it is in the use and power of language.

Steyn explains that historically, moral concern for sexual activity between two persons of the same sex was identified as sodomy, an *act.* And an act is what it is. You can either think it is a good idea or you can think it is bad. Either way, it's very objective. It's what someone does. Then, Steyn explains, in the late nineteenth century the act was redescribed as a *condition* of certain persons, and it was termed "homosexuality"—a condition a person is in. Next, a few decades ago homosexuality got upgraded again, now referring to a person's very *identity,* so that we now identify people as being or not being "gay." Now it describes *who* a person is. Steyn explains:

> Each formulation raises the stakes: One can object to and even criminalize an act; one is obligated to be sympathetic toward a condition; but once it's a fully-fledged 24/7 identity, like being Hispanic or Inuit, anything less than wholehearted acceptance gets you marked down as a bigot.[2]

---

[2]Mark Steyn, "There's No Stopping Them Now," *Chicago Sun-Times,* July 13, 2003, p. 35.

This is where so many good people get stuck. If being gay is a person's identity, how can you object to what they *do* without objecting to who they *are*? We find ourselves torn between our desire to treat other people as we would want to be treated, the golden rule, and our uncomfortableness with homosexuality. Thus we seem to have one foot on the dock and the other on the boat heading out for sea.

But discomfort with opening marriage and parenting to same-sex couples does not equal bigotry! You need go no further for proof of this than the fact that there are homosexuals themselves who do not support the idea of same-sex marriage. They are not driven by hatred for homosexuals but rather by the belief that marriage cannot be bent into anything someone desires it to be.

For example, consider Paul Nathanson, a professor and gay man from McGill University. In a paper he coauthored on why same-sex marriage is not a good idea, he says:

> Every society has found it necessary—whether formally or informally, directly or indirectly—to reward some forms of behavior and either not reward or punish others. . . . [B]ecause heterosexual bonding is directly related to both reproduction and survival; and because it involves much more than copulation, every human society has had to encourage heterosexual bonding actively. Heterosexual bonding is always encouraged by a cultural norm, in other words, not merely allowed as one "lifestyle choice" among many.[3]

This is the substance of Professor Nathanson's case for why same-sex marriage is not a good idea. He is not alone. There are many more homosexuals who oppose same-sex marriage because it doesn't fit with their belief about marriage.[4] Dr. Nathanson and his peers aren't bigots. Someone who shares his convictions need not be either.

---

[3]Katherine Young and Paul Nathanson, "Marriage a la Mode: Answering Advocates of Gay Marriage," (paper presented at the Sex, Marriage, and Family & The Religions of the Book Conference, Center for the Interdisciplinary Study of Religion, Emory University, Atlanta, Ga., April 28, 2003), p. 2. <www.family.org.au/journal/2003/j20030703.html>.

[4]Jim Rinnert, "The Trouble with Gay Marriage," *In These Times*, December 30, 2003, <http://inthesetimes.com/comments.php?id=502_0_3_0_C>.

WHAT THIS ISSUE *IS* ABOUT

In fact, this issue is not even about homosexuals or homosexuality at all. It is about the very nature of marriage. We must ask

- whether we have the right (or ability!) to redefine marriage so it is elastic enough to include any grouping of adults, regardless of gender
- whether a husband and wife need each other
- whether mother and father are both essential in the process of healthy child development
- whether being male or female means anything substantive beyond just body parts and sexual preference
- whether there are compelling societal reasons to define marriage as one thing and not as another
- what the public purpose of marriage is

Each of these questions will be answered throughout this book. We will show there are indeed very deep and compelling reasons to exclusively define marriage as between a man and a woman. With that understood, let's start by examining and answering the central claims of those who advocate redefining marriage to include same-sex partners.

ANSWERING THE SAME-SEX MARRIAGE PROPONENTS

Growing pressure to approve same-sex marriage is everywhere. If same-sex couples are not yet marrying in your state, you can be sure there will be increasing numbers who have married in other states and who will be returning to your home state. Then they will be suing in court for their marriage to be recognized there. *This issue is coming to all of us.*

No doubt you have discussed the issue at work, with your neighbors or even in your family. Perhaps your church denomination has even raised the question. It is possible someone you know and care about is considering entering a same-sex union. Will you know how to respond to these relationships with intelligence and grace?

On the surface, many claims by same-sex marriage proponents seem to be reasonable. But if you dig deeper into these reasons, you find they don't hold up so well. How, as a citizen, do you answer the case for legalizing and normalizing same-sex marriage? In this first section we will address this question. Let's explore some of the most popular justifications for redefining marriage and get at the truth behind them.

1

WHAT'S WRONG WITH
LETTING HOMOSEXUALS MARRY?

You're at lunch with a coworker who is openly homosexual. You've worked together for a few years, and this person has become a genuine friend. You've never felt threatened. He's a good coworker and a cherished friend, and he's always been respectful to you. You have tried to respect him. Still, you're a little surprised when he tells you that he and his partner are thinking of going to Provincetown, Massachusetts, to get married, because homosexual unions are legal there. You sense he is hoping you will be able to celebrate his wedding with him.

He hasn't really asked you about it because he knows you are "way conservative" as he puts it, but he's waiting for your response. What should you say? Is there a way to disagree with him while still affirming him as your friend?

This creates a serious dilemma for you because of conflicting feelings. You care for your friend who lives a life that is different from yours. But you also hold some strong beliefs about marriage, and it seems as if he's asking you—even if not directly—to choose between the two: the regard you have for him and the conviction you have about marriage.

This is a dilemma many of us face—or will face. How do we defend our beliefs about marriage in a thoughtful, caring way, while not feeling like we are attacking our friend? It is important to know that the dilemma is only apparent. You can defend marriage and still affirm a friend with whom you disagree.

Let's begin exploring how to handle this problem.

QUESTION 1. *What's wrong with same-sex marriage?*

ANSWER. Affirming same-sex marriage would forever alter the meaning of marriage and family for everyone.

Marriage is and always has been about bringing men and women together in permanent, exclusive domestic and sexual relationships. No human society—not one—has ever embraced homosexual marriage. It is not a part of the tradition of any human culture.[1] Only until the last few "nanoseconds" of history and experience have societies allowed it.[2] Homosexual unions, married or otherwise, have never been regarded as a *normal, morally equal* part of any society. Nonmarital same-sex unions have been tolerated in some places at some times to be sure but have never been taken to be *morally equivalent* to natural marriage.

This is exactly what is being argued for today. Each of us is being asked to let go of our definition and understanding of marriage and family. We are all being asked to see same-sex marriage as morally and socially equal to natural marriage and this is impossible to do.

QUESTION 2. *Does it really matter how we define marriage?*

ANSWER. It matters in many deep ways. No society has ever allowed a "suit yourself" approach to family, where people choose to live in whatever relationships seem to work for them. All societies need people to live within specific parameters regarding marriage. This is why natural marriage is humanly universal. God has weaved marriage into human nature so that it serves two primary purposes throughout all societies:

• Marriage always brings male and female adults together into committed sexual and domestic relationships in order to regulate sexuality and provide for the needs of daily life. Wives help men channel their sexual energy in socially productive and nonpredatory ways. Husbands help protect women from the exploitation of other males.

• Marriage ensures that children have the benefits of both their mother and their father, each in their distinctive and unique ways.

Together, these two aspects of marriage have been the means by which

---

[1] Some people argue that there have been examples of homosexual marriage in some societies, but this is not true. This topic is addressed in greater detail in chapter three.

[2] Only Canada, Belgium, the Netherlands and Massachusetts have legalized various forms of homosexual marriage in the last few years.

we build strong human communities, generation after generation. As anthropologists tell us, these primary needs shape the family and social norms for all known societies.[3]

Same-sex relationships cannot provide these benefits. These unions provide no essential social good; instead they primarily address the personal or emotional needs and desires of consenting adults. In addition a growing number of these couples want access to the legal and financial benefits granted to those whom society recognizes as married.

One of our nation's most eminent political scientists and social thinkers, James Q. Wilson, brings clarity to what all societies need marriage to do:

> [T]he purpose of marriage . . . has always been to make the family secure, not to redefine what constitutes a family. The family is a more fundamental social reality than a marriage, and so pretending that anything we call a marriage can create a family is misleading. . . . By family, I mean a lasting, socially enforced obligation between a man and a woman that authorizes sexual congress and the supervision of children. . . . There is no society where women alone care for each other and their children; there is none where fathers are not obligated to support their children and the mothers to whom they were born. Not only do men need women, women need men.[4]

That is how God designed us, each for the other: male complements female and female complements male. Marriage is not the only place where males and females do this, but it is the primary place. This whole question comes down to this universal human truth: males and females need each other. However, the same-sex advocates want us to pretend God's design doesn't matter. They want us to believe that males and females are optional

---

[3]Suzanne G. Frayser, *Varieties of Sexual Experience: An Anthropological Perspective on Human Sexuality* (New Haven, Conn.: Human Relations Area Files Press, 1985); Edward Westermarck, *The History of Human Marriage*, vols. 1-3 (New York: Allerton, 1922); Helen E. Fisher, *Anatomy of Love: The Natural History of Monogamy, Adultery and Divorce* (New York: W. W. Norton, 1992); George P. Murdock, *Social Structure* (New York: Macmillan, 1949).
[4]James Q. Wilson, *The Marriage Problem: How Our Culture Has Weakened Families* (New York: Harper Collins, 2002), pp. 24, 29.

and interchangeable. This is a poor view of humanity.

Since marriage is always heterosexual, everywhere, at all times in history, we must ask what has driven this universal constancy of heterosexuality in marriage. The Catholic Church? Jerry Falwell? Dr. Dobson? The Republicans? Western civilization? Dr. Laura? Of course not!

Marriage has not been "imposed" on culture by any religious institution, government, or any other authoritarian power structure from which it must be "set free." God, the architect and builder of nature, established marriage, enforces it by nature—and we tamper with it at our own peril.

QUESTION 3. *Shouldn't two people who love each other be allowed to commit themselves to one another?*

ANSWER. Yes, but we don't always call it marriage. Parents commit themselves to their children, but they aren't married. Friends love and commit themselves to each other, but they aren't married. Coworkers, athletes and soldiers can even love each other and enjoy great commitment, but we don't call it marriage.

Marriage is about a whole lot more than love and commitment. It is not less than these things, to be sure, but it is certainly much more.

Marriage is built on a paradox of humanity—that we exist as male and female. The strong benefit of marriage is that males and females are designed with profound differences, and these differences are coordinated in marriage so that each contributes what the other lacks.[5] Together they create something larger than themselves. The polarity of the two genders is inextricably locked into the meaning and practice of marriage.

We can illustrate this gender complementarity with some simple examples. Think of an electrical plug and a socket or the two electrical poles on a battery. Two positive battery poles produce no electricity. Two sockets by themselves do nothing to serve the electrical needs of your house. A socket must be joined with a plug to make anything meaningful happen.

By themselves, a violin and a bow can't do much. Two bows together can't create any music but rather *mirror* each other because they are the

---

[5]Steven E. Rhoads, *Taking Sex Differences Seriously* (San Francisco: Encounter Books, 2004).

same. They don't complement one another. But together, in their differences, violin and bow create something far greater than they can alone. It's much the same with the two parts of humanity: male and female. Marriage is the coming together of the two different parts to make a whole. Same-sex unions do not make a human whole; they are missing a necessary human ingredient: either male or female.

The benefit of male and female in marriage is not confined to reproduction. The complement and exchange between the sexes provides huge and irreplaceable benefits for both males and females because these differences are rooted in every part of our being. Male and female are not interchangeable human parts. Love and commitment are necessary, but they are not sufficient to form a marriage. Marriage requires persons of different sexes to love and commit themselves to each other.

Besides, couldn't the "people should be able to marry who they love" argument be made for nearly any kind of union? If this is the new criteria for allowing people to marry, how can we say no to a woman who loves a polygamist and wants to become his third wife? How do we say no to Jonathan Yarbrough and Cody Rogahn, the first couple to get a same-sex marriage license in Provincetown, Massachusetts, on May 17, 2004? Yarbrough, a bisexual, said to the press just before his wedding, "I think it's possible to love more than one person and have more than one partner. . . . In our case, we have an open marriage."[6] So what if this couple wanted to expand their open marriage to include some of these other people they plan to love? How would we—how could we—say no? On what basis could we rule out incest, condoning sexual relations and marriage between, say, a loving mother and her adoring son who are both consenting adults?

QUESTION 4. *Why restrict marriage to two persons of different gender, as long as it's restricted to two adults who love each other and are not closely related biologically?*

ANSWER. While you're rejecting one standard of marriage—male and female—you're holding on to another: that it's only about two people. If love and

---

[6]Franci Richardson, "P'town Ready for the 'Big Day,'" *Boston Herald*, May 17, 2004.

commitment were the only criteria for marriage, then not only would concern for gender be eliminated but so would the concern over the number of people in a marriage and their biological relationship. We agree that these kinds of limits to marriage are legitimate and that in maintaining them no one's rights are being violated. Marriage naturally brings with it its own demands. These are what make it marriage. Without them, marriage becomes something else.

Actually there is more of a human-experience case for the gender limit than the number limit. Marriage has always been between men and women in *all* cultures, but it has not always been between two people. Many societies throughout history and the world have practiced polygamy. However, most developed nations enforce a system of male-female monogamy.

But this brings us back to the original question: If marriage is simply about people who love each other and gender doesn't matter for marriage and the family, why does the number of spouses? What criteria will we have for limiting couples like Misters Yarbrough and Rogahn who wish to expand the size of their open marriage to include any of the other people they could fall in love with? What about the gay or lesbian couples who want to "marry" their opposite sex sperm donors in order to make a "complete" family? The question is much more than a rhetorical countermove. In fact, Stanley Kurtz, a research fellow at the Hoover Institution, argues that the "slippery slope" from gay to group marriage is very real and well-greased. He warns:

> The bottom of the slope is visible from where we stand. Advocacy of legalized polygamy is growing. A network of grass-roots organizations seeking legal recognition for group marriage already exists. . . . Actually, there are now many such organizations. And their strategy—even their existence—owes much to the movement for gay marriage.[7]

Kurtz warns that revolutionaries who call themselves "polyamorists" are also capitalizing on the gains won by the same-sex marriage advocates and are ready to make the "love and commitment/justice and equality" case for their idea of marriage.

---

[7]Stanley Kurtz, "Beyond Gay Marriage," *The Weekly Standard*, August 4, 2003, p. 26.

QUESTION 5. *What is polyamory?*

ANSWER. *Polyamory* refers to group marriage. This is different from *polygamy*, where a man takes many wives. Polyamory has been around for a while; its roots are found in the utopian Oneida Community of New York, founded in the mid 1800s. This large but short-lived community of men and women lived as a married group, openly sharing work, homes, children and their beds.[8] Polyamory was continued in some of the hippie communes of the 1960s and early 1970s. Any skeptics of the current vibrancy of the polyamory movement should Google the word *polyamory* and see how much serious support there is for this phenomenon. Kurtz explains that "polyamorists are enthusiastic proponents of same-sex marriage."[9] If the same-sex advocates are successful in abolishing the idea that marriage is only between one man and one woman, then the hard part of making the group marriage case is done. As same-sex advocates make a way for the never-before tolerated definition of homosexual marriage, then it will be easy to usher in multiple-spouse marriages because all that is required in this definition of marriage is the verbal declaration of love and some kind of commitment to someone, anyone. We wager the speed by which this will happen will be swift.

QUESTION 6. *What's the real problem with group or polygamous marriage?*

ANSWER. It would raise a whole new group of issues. If marriage breaks free and overflows its natural boundaries, conforming only to the personal preferences of individuals, then it will lose any definite shape and flood out of control. Marriage will mean what any individual or group wants it to mean, and there will be little social agreement. For all the other problems, expanding marriage beyond a man and woman to all those who want legal acknowledgment of their public declaration of love will force government and industry to provide health and legal benefits for *any* grouping of people who "marry" under these new laws. Can your business afford healthcare benefits

---

[8]Frayser, *Varieties of Sexual Experience,* p. 369.
[9]Kurtz, "Beyond Gay Marriage," p. 28.

for five or nine people in a group marriage? In fact, what will keep two—or four or five—heterosexual, single moms from "marrying" for a time simply so they can receive family health, tax and social security benefits? The increased cost to business and government would be crippling. If any persons who make a public declaration of love are given the right to be legally married, then marriage will cease to have any widely shared meaning within that society. We will be left with socially meaningless, legal ties that bind very little of social value.

Defining marriage on the basis of legally recognized declarations of love may seem harmless, but such subjective expansions of marriage have serious consequences. For example, in nonmonogamous and polygamous societies women typically become commodities to be collected. Only 0.5 percent of all polygamous cultures are polyandrous (one woman, many husbands).[10] Polygamous cultures tend *not* to produce strong, confident women who make important public contributions to the culture. The opposite is true in monogamous cultures.

Anthropologically, socially enforced monogamy tends to socialize male sexual energy and masculinity and protect women from becoming sexual and domestic-service objects to be collected and used by men.[11] The benefits of this counterbalancing arrangement is fully acknowledged in Christianity. God gave Adam a mate to stand by his side to be his helper. He didn't give Adam another guy to hang out with. He gave him a woman, Eve. And not a whole bunch of women. Just one. And Genesis 1:27 tells us she bore God's image along with Adam. *This truth is the most powerful statement of gender equality in all of human thought.* It is impossible to justify treating anyone—man or woman—who bears God's image merely as an object or second-class citizen. And while Christian cultures have not always obeyed this truth, it is a fundamental teaching of Christianity. Marriage is how this equal cooperation between two different and complementary humans (God's unique image bearers) is most fully expressed. However, multipartner and

---

[10]Fisher, *Anatomy of Love,* p. 69.
[11]Frayser, *Varieties of Sexual Experience;* Fisher, *Anatomy of Love;* Murdock, *Social Structure.*

same-sex marriage denies this glorious God-given truth about humanity. Multipartner relationships not only displace monogamy but tilt the table of gender equality in men's favor, while same-sex marriages make either gender irrelevant.

Marriage is also about giving every child a loving and (ideally) biologically connected and committed mother and father. Marriage is how societies promote this complementary nurturing environment for children. It's that simple.

QUESTION 7. *But what about couples who are childless? We let them marry.*

ANSWER. Sterility is the exception and not the rule for heterosexual couples. We do not disqualify couples from marrying based on exceptions that are (for the most part) unanticipated. Many of these couples adopt, lovingly giving a mother and father to a child who needs them. Same-sex couples cannot provide this.

However, sterility is a fully known and inherent part of homosexuality, and therefore children can never come from a homosexual union. Homosexual couples must always go knocking at the door of heterosexuality in order to acquire kids via adoption, artificial insemination or surrogacy.

No one who considers him- or herself homosexual was given life as a result of a homosexual relationship. Everyone enters humanity through the gate of heterosexuality, with the union of male sperm and female egg being the mandatory portal. Homosexuality can never produce people, and it obscures the truth of what is required for human reproduction and development. That is why no society has ever recognized it as a legitimate form of family. It also denies every child it touches what the adults in the relationship had: a mother and father.

QUESTION 8. *But don't we allow older people who are past childbearing years to marry?*

ANSWER. Yes, of course we allow older folks to marry. Having babies is not a requirement of marriage. But it is the expected norm. Older couples marrying is another exception and not a norm. Same-sex marriage advocates are not arguing for their marriage as occasional exceptions but as normal as natural marriage. As leading same-sex activist Evan Wolfson explains, "What we want is not separate and unequal 'gay marriage' but marriage itself, the full range of choices and protections available to our nongay sisters and brothers."[12]

Remember also, the key societal benefit of marriage is not only about bringing forth and raising children but that it brings the genders together into a humanly complete and cooperative relationship. Marriage helps older people complete each other also, and this is good for the individuals and for society.

QUESTION 9. *Why do you have to be so narrow in your definition of marriage?*

ANSWER. Because nature is narrow in its definition of marriage, and for very good reason.

Research over the last one hundred years consistently shows us that marriage provides a treasure chest of good things for adults, children and society (see chapters 8-9). That is why it serves as the foundation of family in all civilizations. As stable marriage has decreased over the past thirty years with dramatic increases in divorce, cohabitation and fatherlessness, the benefits marriage provides have declined as well. Adults and children have been deeply hurt by the decline of marriage. This has been remarkably well-documented, and the evidence is too large and too conclusive to ignore.[13]

Nature does not tolerate very much diversity in the form of family, and any attempt to redefine marriage will be to our detriment. No society has ever prospered under a smorgasbord mentality of family life where people pick and choose forms that suit their individual tastes. To protect the common good, societies must enforce the narrow parameters nature has given humans. Same-sex marriage will simply be the next chapter in a long line of failed social experiments with marriage and the family that have hurt peo-

---

[12]Evan Wolfson, "All Together Now: A Blueprint for Winning the Freedom to Marry," *The Advocate,* September 11, 2001.

[13]Summaries of this mountain of research are found in Glenn T. Stanton, *Why Marriage Matters: Reasons to Believe in Marriage in Postmodern Society* (Colorado Springs: Pinon, 1997); Linda Waite and Maggie Gallagher, *The Case for Marriage* (New York: Doubleday, 2000).

ple. The truth is that anything which deviates from the permanence and health of natural marriage—whether initiated by heterosexuals or homosexuals—is bad for families, children and our whole society, and love of neighbor says we must resist that which is bad for people.

CONCLUSION

Same-sex marriage does not allow more people access to marriage but actually redefines marriage and the family for everyone. It says the complementarity of husband and wife, mother and father are merely optional. Male and female are meaningless, interchangeable parts. Same-sex marriage turns marriage into something it has never been in any other human civilization at any time in history. Natural marriage comprises much more than love between people and access to legal and health benefits. The same-sex proposition robs marriage of its unique virtue in bringing men and women into a cooperative relationship where they complete one another in their differences. Every natural, monogamous marriage is a declaration to all in society that male and female matter.

Marriage is also the best way to ensure that children grow up with a mother and father. But same-sex marriage advocates say none of that matters, and they want to forever change everyone's understanding of marriage and family. What is more, the argument the same-sex advocates use is the same argument that will make way for any type of "marriage." The impact this will have on children, women, business and the government will be staggering.

All societies at all times have limited marriage to be between men and women. What makes us think we don't need it? What makes us so sure we have the ability or the right to alter a fundamental structure and part of the basic meaning of human existence?

2

ISN'T THIS PRIMARILY AN ISSUE OF JUSTICE?

I (Glenn) have two friends who live in the Dakotas. They love each other, have built a life together and plan to live the rest of their lives this way. They would love to get married, but they can't. They are men. Martin asks me, "If you and Jackie can marry and build a life together, why can't Frank and I? We are American citizens just like you. Doesn't justice and the equal protection clause of the U.S. Constitution guarantee us the right to marry?"

As friends, I want Martin and Frank to be happy. As fellow humans and citizens, I want them to be treated with the fullest dignity and respect. But can their desires and my concerns warrant a redefinition of marriage? Does my regard for Martin and Frank, not to mention my commitment to justice, demand I allow for this redefinition? Even if it did somehow help them and my relationship with them, would such a redefinition serve the needs of our whole society? I am not the only one who struggles with this. Many people have friends and loved ones who desire to enter same-sex marriages. In this chapter we explore whether justice is being served by how we define marriage.

QUESTION 1. *But surely gays have the same right to marry as heterosexuals, don't they?*

ANSWER. Let's be very clear. Homosexuals *do* have the constitutional right to marry. But no one has a right to redefine marriage for themselves or for a whole society. No one has a right to say male and female, mothers and fathers, don't matter for society and the family. But this is exactly what giving social and legal sanction to same-sex marriage would do.

Many homosexuals have indeed married members of the opposite sex, and no homosexual has ever charged any state or federal government with barring him or her from marrying because of their own sexual preference. It has never happened. The state is blind to such matters of personal orienta-tion. There are some very basic legal parameters as to who any of us can marry, and they apply equally to all of us. This satisfies the "equal protec-tion" clause of the Fourteenth Amendment. Traditionally, when any of us seeks a marriage license, we

- can't already be married
- must be an adult and must marry an adult
- can't marry a close family member
- must marry someone of the opposite sex

Now if two people meeting all these criteria go to city hall to get a marriage license, and the clerk asks whether either are homosexual and denies them a marriage license based on an affirmative answer, that would be discriminatory. Current law does not keep homosexual individuals from marrying. It just keeps them—as well as heterosexuals—from redefining marriage by marrying a person of the same sex. Our current marriage laws treat everyone equally.

This debate isn't about equality or access to marriage; it's about *redefining* marriage, making it something it has never been before.

QUESTION 2. *Heterosexuals can marry according to their sexual orienta-tion. Why shouldn't homosexuals be allowed to marry according to their orientation?*

ANSWER. This argument compares apples with oranges. The assertion rests on an immense, unproven theory that homosexuality is rooted in nature just as heterosexuality is.

Historically, heterosexuality has never been considered an orientation. It was only when homosexuality gained political legitimacy that we started re-ferring to sexual "orientations." People have always been understood to be heterosexual even if some people want to have sex with members of the same sex. Being *gay* is more of a political description than a psychosexual one. And it is a relatively new term. Marriage has never been defined or reg-ulated according to orientation, one way or another.

Besides, no United States court has ever recognized and no scientific institution anywhere in the world has ever established the immutability (i.e., qualities we are born with and therefore cannot change) of homosexuality. Many scientists have tried, but none has ever succeeded. Homosexuality cannot be compared to genealogy or ethnic heritage, which cannot be changed any more than the past can be changed.

In the early 1990s, Columbia University researchers William Byne and Bruce Parsons carefully analyzed all the major biological studies on homosexuality. Finding no studies that supported a purely biological cause for homosexuality, they found the origins of homosexual identification rooted in a "complex mosaic of biologic, psychological and social/cultural factors."[1] More recently, Professors Richard Friedman and Jennifer Downey, writing on the nature of sexual orientation, explain:

> At clinical conferences one often hears that homosexual orientation is fixed and unmodifiable. Neither assertion is true. . . . [T]he assertion that homosexuality is genetic is so reductionistic that it must be dismissed out of hand as a general principle of psychology.[2]

Therefore, it is wrong to assert that heterosexual and homosexual orientations are essentially the same and should therefore be treated equally. One is firmly rooted in nature and as a result is manifest as the foundation of all human civilizations. The other is far less common and the result of influences that are little understood and not intrinsic to human nature.[3]

QUESTION 3. *But isn't this fundamentally a question of equality?*

ANSWER. The implied answer to this question may seem persuasive because all of us favor equality—and few of us are fans of inequality. But before we answer, there are a number of vital facts we need to be mindful of.

First, marriage is not about equality. Marriage is about setting norms for

---

[1]William Byne and Bruce Parsons, "Human Sexual Orientation: The Biologic Theories Reappraised," *Archives of General Psychiatry* 50 (1993): 228-39.

[2]Richard C. Friedman and Jennifer I. Downey, *Sexual Orientation and Psychoanalysis: Sexual Science and Clinical Practice* (New York: Columbia University Press, 2002), p. 39.

[3]We will address the "naturalness" of homosexuality more fully in chap. 13.

society for how we structure sexual relationships, for creating cooperative and respectful domestic relationships between the sexes, and for forming families for raising children. Anthropologist Suzanne Frayser, after studying the role marriage plays across diverse civilizations, offers this universal definition: "Marriage is a relationship within which a group socially approves and encourages sexual intercourse and the birth of children."[4] Edward Westermarck, who has written an immense three-volume history of human marriage, agrees. He says marriage is always about bringing forth the next generation.[5]

Prominent gay activists clearly admit that this is not a question of "equality." They are not shy of letting us know it's about something else. For example, Michelangelo Signorile explains in *OUT* magazine, a leading voice in the gay community, that

> The trick is, gay leaders and pundits must stop watering the issue down—"this is simply about equality for gay couples"—and offer same-sex marriage for what it is: an opportunity to reconstruct a traditionally homophobic institution by bringing it to our more equitable queer value system, . . . a chance to wholly transform the definition of family in American culture. . . . Our gay leaders must acknowledge that gay marriage is just as *radical* and *transformative* as the religious Right contends it is.[6]

QUESTION 4. *But doesn't our drive toward equality essentially demand same-sex marriage?*

ANSWER. Not at all. Humanity has benefited from a very robust discussion of equality, liberty and freedom for many centuries. Think of the brightest minds and most articulate voices here: John Stuart Mill, Frederick Douglass, Thomas Jefferson, Elizabeth Cady Stanton, Susan B. Anthony, Mohandas

---

[4]Suzanne G. Frayser, *Varieties of Sexual Experience: An Anthropological Perspective on Human Sexuality* (New Haven, Conn.: Human Relations Area Files Press, 1985), p. 248.
[5]Edward Westermarck, *The History of Human Marriage*, vols. 1-3 (New York: Allerton, 1922).
[6]Michelangelo Signorile, "I DO, I DO, I DO, I DO, I DO," *OUT*, May 1996, pp. 30, 32 (emphasis in original).

Gandhi, the Rev. Dr. Martin Luther King Jr. None of them ever hinted that the fact that marriage exists exclusively as the union of male and female is an impediment to human equality.

In his great "I Have a Dream!" speech, Dr. King, the most contemporary and modern mind in the above list, did not proclaim, "I envision a day when couples will be judged by the depth of their love rather than the make-up of their gender." If same-sex marriage is such a *basic and fundamental* human right (as the Massachusetts Supreme Judicial Court declared in its *Goodridge* decision), why did he and all those great visionaries before him fail to see it?

None of these great civil rights leaders ever advocated for same-sex marriage as a fundamental human right because it *isn't* a fundamental human right. Instead, the "equality" argument was deliberately picked up by the gay political community as a rhetorical device to gain advantage among those outside of their constituency. Michelangelo Signorile goes on to explain in his essay that "freedom to marry" was "actually something that activists began using on the advice of a Los Angeles PR firm, based on how well they believed it would play in the heterosexual mainstream."[7]

QUESTION 5. *Isn't banning gay marriage just like banning interracial marriage?*

ANSWER. They are nothing alike.

Bans on interracial marriage were designed to keep races apart, and that was and is wrong. The historic definition of marriage is rooted in bringing the genders together, which is good. Race is not a fundamental quality or aspect of marriage. But gender is.

Therefore, allowing interracial marriage did not call for a *redefinition* but rather an *affirmation* of marriage. It says males should be able to marry females, regardless of race. Same-sex marriage is something very different—a redefinition of marriage.

It's a very different thing for a child to say that "I have a Caucasian

---

[7]Ibid., p. 32.

mother and an Asian father" than "I have two dads and no mother." There is no research saying biracial parents are developmentally harmful to children. But there are thousands of definitive studies showing motherless and fatherless families limit every important measure of children's physical, psychological, emotional and intellectual development.[8] Not only do the social sciences show that fatherless and motherless families are harmful to children (which every same-sex home suffers from), but they also show that stepfamilies where a child's mother or father is replaced by a stepmother or stepfather (which constitute many—if not most—same-sex homes) are some of the most troubling family forms for children. In im-

---

[8]Many of these studies are either presented or represented in David Popenoe, *Life Without Father: Compelling Evidence That Fatherhood and Marriage Are Indispensable for the Good of Children* (New York: Free Press, 1996); Glenn T. Stanton, *Why Marriage Matters: Reasons to Believe in Marriage in Postmodern Society* (Colorado Springs: Pinon Press, 1997); Ronald P. Rohner and Robert A. Veneziano, "The Importance of Father Love: History and Contemporary Evidence," *Review of General Psychology* 5, no. 4 (2001): 382-405; Kyle D. Pruett, *Fatherneed: Why Father Care Is as Essential as Mother Care for Your Child* (New York: Free Press, 2000); David Blankenhorn, *Fatherless America: Confronting Our Most Urgent Social Problem* (New York: Basic Books, 1994); Sara McLanahan and Gary Sandefur, *Growing Up with a Single Parent: What Hurts, What Helps* (Cambridge, Mass.: Harvard University Press, 1994); Ellen Bing, "The Effect of Child-Rearing Practices on the Development of Differential Cognitive Abilities," *Child Development* 34 (1963): 631-48; Deborah Dawson, "Family Structure and Children's Health and Well-Being: Data from the 1988 National Health Interview Survey on Child Health," *Journal of Marriage and the Family* 53 (1991): 573-84; Scott Coltrane, "Father-Child Relationships and the Status of Women: A Cross-Cultural Study," *American Journal of Sociology* 93 (1988): 1088; Michael Gottfredson and Travis Hirschi, *A General Theory of Crime* (Stanford, Calif.: Stanford University Press, 1990), p. 103; Richard Koestner et al., "The Family Origins of Empathic Concern: A Twenty-Six Year Longitudinal Study," *Journal of Personality and Social Psychology* 58 (1990): 709-17; E. Mavis Hetherington, "Effects of Father Absence on Personality Development in Adolescent Daughters," *Developmental Psychology* 7 (1972): 313-26; Irwin Garfinkel and Sara McLanahan, *Single Mothers and Their Children: A New American Dilemma* (Washington, D.C.: Urban Institute Press, 1986), pp. 30-31; Sara McLanahan, "Life Without Father: What Happens to Children?" Center for Research on Child Well-Being Working Paper 01-21 (Princeton, N.J.: Princeton University, 2001); Paul R. Amato and Fernando Rivera, "Paternal Involvement and Children's Behavior Problems," *Journal of Marriage and the Family* 61 (1999): 375-84; David Ellwood, *Poor Support: Poverty in the American Family* (New York: Basic Books, 1988), p. 46; Ronald J. Angel and Jacqueline Worobey, "Single Motherhood and Children's Health," *Journal of Health and Social Behavior* 29 (1988): 38-52; L. Remez, "Children Who Don't Live with Both Parents Face Behavioral Problems," *Family Planning Perspectives*, January-February 1992; Judith Wallerstein et al., *The Unexpected Legacy of Divorce: A 25 Year Landmark Study* (New York: Hyperion, 2000); Nicholas Zill, Donna Morrison and Mary Jo Coiro, "Long-Term Effects of Parental Divorce on Parent-Child Relationships, Adjustment, and Achievement in Young Adulthood," *Journal of Family Psychology* 7 (1993): 91-103.

portant ways this is more troubling than even single parent homes.[9]

Being of a particular race is nothing like having homosexual desire. Again, no academic institution in the world nor any U.S. court has ever established that homosexuality is given at birth and is a permanent feature of an individual like race, nationality and gender are. There are no former Blacks, Whites, Hispanics or Asian folks. But there are hundreds of people documented who have happily and successfully left homosexuality.[10] Homosexuality and race are clearly two different things and therefore should not be treated as similar.

This same question was presented to the Supreme Court of Minnesota, which ruled in 1971 that race and homosexuality are *not* similar. Based on *Loving v. Virginia*, the 1967 U.S. Supreme Court case striking down state bans on interracial marriage, the Minnesota court said:

> *Loving* does indicate that not all state restrictions upon the right to marry are beyond reach of the Fourteenth Amendment. But in commonsense and in a constitutional sense, there is a clear distinction between a marital restriction based merely on race and one based on the fundamental difference in sex.[11]

The case was appealed to the United States Supreme Court, which refused to hear it, citing "appeal dismissed for want of a substantial federal question."[12] The highest court in our land apparently did not view the race-homosexuality comparison as a serious constitutional question.

---

[9]For instance, one respected family socialist explains, "Social scientists used to believe that, for positive child outcomes, stepfamilies were preferable to single-parent families. Today, we are not so sure. Stepfamilies typically have an economic advantage, but some recent studies indicate that the children of stepfamilies have as many behavioral and emotional problems as the children of single-parent families, and possibly more" (David Popenoe, "The Evolution of Marriage and the Problem of Stepfamilies: A Biosocial Perspective," in *Stepfamilies: Who Benefits? Who Does Not?* ed. Alan Booth and Judy Dunn [Hillsdale, N.J.: Lawrence Erlbaum Associates, 1994], p. 5).

[10]Robert L. Spitzer, "Can Some Gay Men and Lesbians Change Their Sexual Orientation? 200 Participants Reporting a Change From Homosexual to Heterosexual Orientation," *Archives of Sexual Behavior*, 32 (2003): 403-17.

[11]*Baker v. Nelson*, Supreme Court of Minnesota, 1971.

[12]*Baker v. Nelson*, 409 U.S. 810 (1972).

The comparison of race and gender really implies that opponents to same-sex marriage are bigots, but this is not true. They simply believe that marriage is for men and women of whatever race.

What is more, polls consistently show African Americans in large numbers oppose same-sex marriage, indicating they don't align themselves with the homosexual movement.[13] Many are deeply offended at the comparison of gay rights with civil rights when used by homosexual activists.[14]

QUESTION 6. *Hasn't society "evolved" beyond exclusive heterosexuality? We certainly live in a different age than we did thirty years ago.*

ANSWER. Even if you have an evolutionary, naturalistic worldview, marriage has been the universal and most efficient creator of a healthy next generation, which is why it is the norm in all human civilizations. It works best for producing and raising the next (healthy) generation of humanity.

Successful evolution would seem to demand that we shouldn't stray from heterosexual bonding. Again, no person who claims to be homosexual came into this world as a result of homosexual coupling. Since a homosexual couple cannot pass on their genes together, homosexuality disqualifies itself as a mechanism for facilitating evolutionary human progress. And it also explains how a genetic disposition toward homosexuality is unlikely. It would have been sucked down the drain of the gene pool long ago due to a very inefficient means of transmission from one generation to another.

QUESTION 7. *Isn't marriage an inherently religious institution that adheres to very narrow prohibitions? Shouldn't marriage be set free from the restrictions of the church?*

ANSWER. When we think of weddings, we think of churches. When we think of marriage licenses, we think of city hall. Both church and state have a stake in marriage. *Churches* are interested in making sure that marriages are healthy and strong. But city hall—as well as both state and federal gov-

---

[13]Ta-Nehisi Coates, "Queer Eye for the Black Guy," *The Village Voice,* September 30, 2003, accessed on June 15, 2004, at <http://www.villagevoice.com/issues/0339/coates.php>.

[14]Alvin Williams, "Blacks Resent Comparison of Gay Rights to Civil Right," *The Charlotte Observer,* April 23, 2004, p. 9A.

ernments—have a huge stake in marriage as well. As Maggie Gallagher explains, "There is scarcely a dollar that state and federal government spends on social programs that is not driven in large part by family fragmentation: crime, poverty, drug abuse, teen pregnancy, school failure, mental and physical health problems."[15]

Marriage provides many benefits for society, like healthier people; more productive, law-abiding citizens; healthier, more well-adjusted children who do better in and complete school, and don't get involved in criminal and antisocial behavior (see chapters 8-9). When marriages fail, they fail to provide those good things essential to healthy society, and the state must prop up the decline. So both church and state do have a stake in marriage, each for their own reasons. Marriage doesn't belong just to religious institutions.

But it is also important to remember that in the history of human culture, marriage didn't arise because some government or religious institution dictated that people *must* marry. Marriage predates both the organized church and the state.[16] God rooted it in all of human nature. Therefore, it isn't the job of either the church or the state to redefine marriage to accommodate the current preferences of some individuals. Rather it is in the interest of both church and state to preserve marriage in its given and natural form. Both must therefore support and champion natural marriage.

But it is significant that every one of the world's major religions (with the exception of Buddhism, which is silent on the issue) has historically held prohibitions against both homosexual sexual relations and unions. The major world religions define marriage as between male and female, and have always had prohibitions against homosexuality. This vast consensus ought to tell us something about the abiding nature of marriage throughout time and across cultures.

QUESTION 8. *Haven't historians of early Christianity found same-sex marriage ceremonies being practiced in ancient Christian times?*

---

[15]Maggie Gallagher, "The Stakes: Why We Need Marriage," *National Review Online,* July 14, 2003, accessed on June 15, 2004, at <http://www.nationalreview.com/comment/comment -gallagher071403.asp>.

[16]Edward Westermarck, *The History of Human Marriage* (New York: Allerton, 1922), 1:27.

ANSWER. There is one historian, John Boswell, who got a good deal of press on this issue in the early 1990s. Asserting that homosexual unions were ritually honored in the medieval Christian church, Boswell got rave reviews from some newspapers and the popular press. But his work on this thesis has not been favorably reviewed by any historian of antiquity.

Boswell explains that the early church practiced ritualized ceremonies in which two men or two women entered into brotherhood and sisterhood relationships. And this is largely true. But Boswell errs when he makes the leap of equating these friendship ceremonies with the recognition and blessing of erotic homosexual relationships.

A professor of early Christian history, panning Boswell's book in the journal *First Things,* explains, "Nine years ago I was joined in devout sisterhood to another woman, apparently in just such a ceremony as Boswell claims to elucidate in his book." She explains the ceremony was performed in the Church of the Holy Sepulchre in Jerusalem by an Orthodox archbishop. The other woman was not the professor's lover but her professional colleague and friend, another professor of history. Upon meeting the women in the midst of their Middle East tour, the archbishop remarked the ladies must be very good friends since they "had survived the rigors of Syria and Eastern Turkey in amicable good humor" and offered a ceremonial blessing on such a special friendship.[17] They were honored to have their sisterhood blessed in such a special way. These friendship ceremonies have long been a part of certain Christian traditions.

The professor goes on to explain that Boswell's scholarship "is studded with unwarranted *a priori* assumptions, with arguments from silence and with dubious, or in some cases outrageously false, translations of critical terms." She warns that Boswell's slipperiness with historical accuracy and principles of interpretation "would be unacceptable in an undergraduate paper." She gives the example where Boswell says, "Certainly the most controversial same-sex couple in the Christian tradition comprised Jesus and John"

---

[17]Robin Darling Young, "Gay Marriage: Reimaging Church History," *First Things* (November 1994), p. 43.

on the basis of Christ calling John his "beloved disciple."[18]

John Boswell cannot be taken seriously as a reasonable historian.

QUESTION 9. *But if most religions object to same-sex marriage, can't we just allow civil same-sex marriages and let churches do what they want?*

ANSWER. We think not. If same-sex marriage is seen as a fundamental human right by the United States Supreme Court—as the Massachusetts Supreme Judicial Court found in its infamous *Goodridge* decision—then all citizens will be forced to recognize it. A just society can't be selective about which groups will recognize fundamental human rights. If they are basic or fundamental, everyone must recognize them.

Only months after legalizing same-sex "marriage" in Canada, activists there successfully passed C-250, a bill criminalizing public statements that could be deemed "hateful" to homosexuals, punishable by up to two years in prison![19] Say the wrong thing; go to jail. Churches in Canada cannot speak against homosexuality without fear of punishment. The same could happen here.

Every public school in the nation, K-12, will no doubt be compelled to teach that same-sex "marriage" and homosexuality are perfectly normal. Pictures and story lines in textbooks also will most likely be changed to show same-sex couples as normal. If the right to same-sex marriage is identical to civil rights, then we should expect the same kind of governmental enforcement of the law.

Your church could very well be pressured to perform same-sex weddings or lose some or all of its privileges. When courts find same-sex marriage to be a constitutional and fundamental human right, the American Civil Liberties Union can convincingly argue that the government is underwriting discrimination by offering tax exemptions to churches and synagogues that only honor natural marriage. It could happen in every state in the union.

Gay and lesbian people have a right to form meaningful relationships. They don't have a right to redefine marriage for all of us. *If same-sex marriage*

[18]Ibid., p. 46.
[19]"A Body Blow to Free Speech," *National Post*, May 19, 2004, p. A21.

is legalized in America, all citizens will be affected by this shift in the civil and religious meaning of marriage. Furthermore, protection of your religious right to live out your faith in public by voicing moral criticism of this arrangement would be seriously eroded if not eliminated.

QUESTION 10. *But some believe that same-sex marriage could actually strengthen the institution of marriage. Isn't this true?*

ANSWER. Wouldn't that be a bit like saying printing counterfeit money would help strengthen the economy by putting more dollars into circulation? Marriage is not the creation of human beings; thus it is not our province to change it. It doesn't thrive under the inclusive banner of "the more the merrier." A marriage culture, which is essential to a healthy society, is nourished when we are faithful to and honor its time-tested definition, which is simply not elastic.

In addition, recent research from a major British medical journal on male same-sex relationships in the Netherlands—arguably one of the most gay-friendly cultures in the world (and where same-sex marriage is legal)—indicates gay men have a very difficult time living by the values of marriage. This study found that, on average, steady homosexual relationships in the city of Amsterdam last only 1.5 years. The study also found that gay men in steady relationships there have an average of eight partners a year outside of their current relationships.[20] And remember the attitude of the first couple in line on May 17, 2004, to get a same-sex marriage license in Provincetown, Massachusetts. They admitted to having an open marriage.

Contrast that with the fact that 67 percent of first marriages in the United States last ten years, and more than three-quarters of heterosexual married couples report being faithful to their wedding vows.[21]

Some same-sex marriage apologists explain that if homosexuals had the

---

[20]Maria Xiridou et al., "The Contributions of Steady and Casual Partnerships to the Incidence of HIV Infection Among Homosexual Men in Amsterdam," *AIDS* 17 (2003): 1029-38.

[21]Matthew Bramlett and William Mosher, "First Marriage Dissolution, Divorce and Remarriage: United States," *Advance Data, National Center for Health Statistics*, May 31, 2001, p. 1; Edward O. Laumann et al., *The Social Organization of Sexuality: Sexual Practices in the United States* (Chicago: University of Chicago Press, 1994), p. 216.

social pull of marriage to keep them monogamous like heterosexuals do, then they would be more monogamous like heterosexuals. But data like that from Amsterdam exposes this as wishful thinking. In addition, an article in *OUT* magazine quotes a thirty-two-year-old gay man as a normative gay voice on the question of the virtue of marriage and monogamy:

> As far as the legalities and financial aspects, yes, I'd definitely get married. But would that make me monogamous? No way. I think it's silly for anyone, straight or gay, to define it that way.[22]

No, opening marriage to people who simply want the legal benefits it provides and little else does not strengthen marriage.

QUESTION 11. *Doesn't our culture benefit from trying new things? Shouldn't we be open to new concepts?*

ANSWER. Thirty years ago our nation entered a dramatic social experiment with the family, with no knowledge of how it would turn out, called "no-fault divorce," thinking this would improve family life. The intervening thirty years of experience and social-science research, however, have judged this experiment a massive failure. Children have been hurt far more deeply—and for much longer—than any of us ever imagined.

The Council on Families in America, a diverse group of America's leading family scholars, declares:

> America's divorce revolution has failed. The evidence of failure is overwhelming. . . . [It] has created terrible hardships for children. It has generated poverty within families. It has burdened us with unsupportable social costs. It has failed to deliver on its promise of greater adult happiness and better relationships between men and women. . . . Too many children are angry, sad, and neglected.[23]

Of our no-fault divorce experiment, pioneering divorce researcher

---

[22]Signorile, "I DO, I DO, I DO, I DO, I DO," p. 113.

[23]*Marriage in America: A Report to the Nation,* Council on Families in America, Institute for American Values, 1995, <www.americanvalues.org/html/r-marriage_in_america.html>.

Dr. Judith Wallerstein also observes:

> We made radical changes in the family without realizing how it changes the experience of growing up. We embarked on a gigantic social experiment without any idea about how the next generation would be affected. If the truth be told, and if we are able to face it, the history of divorce in our society is replete with unwarranted assumptions that adults have made about children simply because such assumptions are congenial to adult needs and wishes.[24]

Given that children were hurt so deeply by a massive social experiment fueled purely by adult preferences, it is foolish to embark on another historically unprecedented and unproven social experiment with our children for the sole intent of meeting adult sexual and emotional desire. *And just as no-fault divorce said "till death do us part" was not important, the same-sex proposition says the husband and wife part of marriage doesn't matter. Why do we think we will not experience the same deep negative consequences if we so radically tinker with marriage again?* Allowing for this experiment would be anything but wise and compassionate.

QUESTION 12. *Surely, though, homosexuals need marriage to feel like full members of society, don't they?*

ANSWER. Need marriage? No. What we are talking about here is the need for self-esteem, and it is not the place of government (much less marriage!) to bestow self-esteem on any individual or group.

Do we walk down the aisle toward marriage to enhance our self-esteem, or is it for some greater, higher purpose: the well-being and completion of the other part of humanity—our new spouse—and the begetting and raising of children? What purpose would homosexual marriage serve beyond mere companionship, which can be had without benefit of the legal standing of marriage? Legal standing, especially in violation of a built-in natural requirement, cannot contribute to someone's self-esteem.

---

[24]Wallerstein, *Unexpected Legacy,* p. xxii.

CONCLUSION

Marriage doesn't serve individuals' or couples' needs for equality and justice before the law. It serves the cultural need for social norms for how we channel sexual energy in socially beneficial ways. Marriage is the way we socialize men, protect women from the exploitation of unattached males and ensure every child grows up with a mother and a father. This is driven by nature, and it is why we find it in every known society and the major world religions.

Allowing same-sex marriage is nothing like allowing interracial marriage. Marriage is not about keeping races apart but bringing male and female together. One is rooted in bigotry and the other is rooted in the nature of what the next generation needs.

We have already entered one experiment with marriage in order to fulfill adult desire. The no-fault divorce revolution changed our understanding of marriage, and it failed miserably in improving human well-being. Why do we think another radical experiment will be any more successful?

There is no civil right to redefine marriage and deny children their mother or father in order to fulfill adults' wishes for same-sex marriage and families. That alternative cannot be considered just nor compassionate.

3

HAVEN'T OTHER CULTURES HAD
SAME-SEX MARRIAGE?

Remember that zoology class we took in college?" Leslie asked. "Remember all the diversity in the animal kingdom, how sometimes males gave birth to the babies and cared for them, while mothers did the work in other species?" She continued, "Why can't humanity, which is so much more developed and adaptive, have the same sort of diversity in how it does family? Why does family have to be male and female only?"

Todd was surprised that he was stumped by Leslie's question. She seemed to question the unquestionable. He had taken some anthropology courses and stayed awake through most of them. He found it interesting to study various human cultures and learn how they lived, the kinds of values and taboos they had as a society and how they structured their lives. In an "anthropology of the family" section during one semester, he remembered that all the cultures they studied had permanent pair-bonding structures between men and women, even if they had different divisions of labor. Were there any cultures that did what Leslie was suggesting? *Maybe humanity could be more like species in the animal kingdom.* It didn't seem right, but he wasn't sure. Having an interest in this area, Todd wished he had an informed, confident answer for his friend.

Maybe you have found yourself struggling with such questions about what human culture requires—and can tolerate—regarding family diversity. Perhaps you have a friend like Leslie whom you respect and want to be able to offer a sound, respectful response to. We will explore many of the most relevant questions on this subject in this chapter.

QUESTION 1. *But haven't there been different kinds of marriage in all kinds of human civilizations?*

ANSWER. Yes and no. We see great diversity in the ways different cultures do family, from the family that lives in a brownstone in Manhattan to those that live in the jungles of New Guinea. But for all the diversity we see, it isn't as diverse as you might think. The main differences among families around the world are (1) number of partners in the marriage and (2) division of labor between male and female.[1]

But if you spun a globe and randomly stabbed your finger down on any inhabited landmass and went there to observe its family model at any time in history, you would find that they do marriage as a heterosexual union between men and women.[2] You would never find one that didn't. There may be other differences, but the nature of marriage bringing male and female together is constant and universal.

QUESTION 2. *I have heard of some societies that have allowed members of the same sex to marry.*

ANSWER. There is not one human society, advanced or primitive, civilized or uncivilized, where homosexual marriage has existed as a normative part of family life. Homosexual marriage hasn't emerged in any human culture until the last few years. It was early in 2001 that the first country on earth legally recognized marriage between same-sex couples.

Let's look at the record of human history.

Early anthropologist Edward Westermarck, author of the groundbreaking, three-volume *History of Human Marriage,* explains that as we examine all human civilizations, we always see some basic characteristics:

> Marriage is generally used as a term for a social institution. Marriage always implies the right to sexual intercourse: society holds such intercourse allowable in the case of husband and wife. . . . At the same time, marriage is something more than a regulated sexual relation. . . . It is the husband's duty . . . to support his wife and children; . . . the

---

[1]Another difference in family formation is worth mentioning but is extremely rare, where husband and wife continue to live with their individual clan groups after marriage. See Edward Westermarck, *The History of Human Marriage* (New York: Allerton, 1922), 1:45.
[2]Ibid., 1:26, 28, 46.

man being the protector and supporter of his family and woman being the helpmate and the nurse of their children. The habit was sanctioned by custom, and afterwards by law, and was thus transformed into a social institution. . . . [T]he functions of the husband and father in the family are not merely the sexual and procreative kind, but involve the duty of protecting the wife and children, is testified by an array of facts relating to peoples in all quarters of the world and in all stages of civilization.[3]

WHO HAS SEXUAL INTERCOURSE?

Webster's New Riverside University Dictionary defines "sexual intercourse" as "n. Coitus, esp. between humans." When we flip to the front of the dictionary we find "Coitus" defined as "n. Physical union of male and female sexual organs." A dictionary is not a legal document, but it conveys a culture's common understanding of what something is, and therefore isn't. Human culture has not seen homoerotic genital stimulation as sexual intercourse. It is something else.

Another celebrated anthropologist, Margaret Mead, illustrates the cultural universality of husband-wife/father-mother pairing in her work *Male and Female:*

When we survey all known human societies, we find everywhere some form of the family, some set of permanent arrangements by which males assist females in caring for children while they are young. . . . [T]here is the assumption of permanent mating, the idea that the marriage should last as long as both live.[4]

And a founding father of anthropology, Bronislaw Malinowski, in *Sex, Culture and Myth* observes:

---

[3]Ibid., 1:27-28.
[4]Margaret Mead, *Male and Female: A Study of the Sexes in a Changing World* (New York: William Morrow, 1949), pp. 188, 195.

In all human societies the father is regarded by tradition as indispens-able. The woman has to be married before she is allowed legitimately to conceive. . . . This is by no means only a European or Christian prej-udice; it is the attitude found amongst most barbarous and savage people as well. . . . The most important moral and legal rule concern-ing the physiological side of kinship is that no child should be brought into the world without a man—and one man at that—assuming the role of sociological father, that is, of guardian and protector, the male link between the child and the rest of the community. (T)his general-ization amounts to a universal sociological law . . . and is indispens-able for the full sociological status of the child as well as of its mother.[5]

QUESTION 3. *But aren't there examples of homosexual marriage in history?*

ANSWER. Some people say that a few societies have experienced same-sex marriages, and that is true in a very narrow sense. But examples are ex-tremely rare and have typically been strange anomalies and never have been normalized as parts of society. You could not walk through villages or towns and observe in one house a man married to a woman and in the house next door a woman married to a woman.

Some powerful kings and rulers have taken mates of the same sex. The most prominent example is the Roman emperor Nero, who along with mar-rying another man also murdered people routinely and appointed a horse to the Senate.

After extensive research throughout a large body of anthropological writ-ings, we have only been able to find two incidents where a culture tolerated some form of same-sex "marriage." As you will see, these two incidents are far from what is being proposed by some activists today and far different from what marriage actually is.

- *Women "marriage" in Dahomey.* In parts of West Africa in the early twenti-eth century, there is an anthropological report of women "marrying" other women. But closer examination reveals the larger picture and context.

---

[5]Bronislaw Malinowski, *Sex, Culture and Myth* (New York: Harcourt, Brace & World, 1962), pp. 62-63.

The anthropologist explains that a "barren woman will formally marry a young girl and hand her over to her husband with a view to bearing children."[6] The younger woman lives in separate quarters, and the relationship between the two women is not sexual or even emotional. It's a business deal. The hiring woman, if she is not married, will pay men to have intercourse with the girl in her quarters in order to bring forth offspring. Rules were established that if the girl runs off with one of her sires, the resultant offspring belongs to the financing woman. These are not homosexual relationships. They are business contracts to produce children.

- *Native American* Berdache. The only other case of such same-sex "marriages" in a culture is found across Native American aboriginal tribes.

Relationships between two men were allowed where one man was seen as a *berdache*: a "part woman-male" or "he-she" male. When these unions developed, they took place with wealthier males and always in the context of an already existent heterosexual—and usually polygamous—marriage that had produced children. A *berdache* did not have an emotional relationship with his "husband" but was a secondary worker-spouse. The *berdache* presented himself as a woman and joined the women in their work. This change from man to woman was attributed to a special vision experienced by the *berdache*.[7]

Two masculine men would never marry, and two *berdache* would not marry. Their roles were never confused. Sex between masculine males was taboo. Sex between a male and his *berdache* was rare and curiously seen as either a spiritual reflection or an object of humor among other male peers. It was never a part of normal tribal life. Males would routinely tease and ridicule other males with *berdaches* because the *berdaches* had reputations of being highly productive workers, eager to please. He could hunt, cook and clean. He did not get distracted from his work with pregnancy, nursing

[6]Melville J. Herskovits, "A Note on 'Woman Marriage' in Dahomey," *Africa* 10 (1937). The article is reprinted in Andrew Sullivan, *Same Sex Marriage: Pro and Con* (New York: Vintage Books, 1997), pp. 32-34.
[7]Suzanne G. Frayser, *Varieties of Sexual Experience: Anthropological Perspective on Human Sexuality* (New York: Human Relations Area File Press, 1985), p. 89.

and childcare. The men would never tease the *berdache* directly, because he was not seen as a man. Among the Mohaves, the kidding could get so bad that many men would send their *berdaches* away to never return.

Long-term sexual relationships with a *berdache* was discouraged. They were seen primarily as workers. In addition, the husband-*berdache* relationships were notoriously unstable. These relationships are nothing like same-sex unions that are being proposed today. No society has ever had anything similar to the contemporary idea of homosexual marriage.

And there are very good reasons why no society has ever done this, and these reasons are not rooted in restrictive religion or authoritarian government but in natural law. (These very compelling reasons why families are always formed by permanent male and female coupling are presented in section two.)

CONCLUSION

All of the family diversity we find throughout all human cultures—such as number of spouses and how the work is divided between men and women—falls in the *heterosexual* category. In very rare cases people of the same sex were given to marriage, but these were relationships where a service was provided. They were not emotional and rarely sexual. Marriage between men and women is the foundation for all human societies. It is more than an emotional relationship created to benefit the individuals in the marriage. Every marriage is a social good, living out a community norm for the common good of the society.

4

How Would Homosexual Marriage Threaten Other Families?

We have come to a place in our world where we are starting to recognize how small, seemingly benign behaviors and activities can have a huge effect on society. Spraying deodorant or hairspray out of an aerosol can can hurt an unseen but essential ozone layer. Killing off the tiny snail darter, the spotted owl or the Amazon rainforest can have a far deeper ecological impact than most of us realize. Dumping your used motor oil in a hole in your backyard can harm the water quality for people next door or across town. We have learned that a particularly unspectacular event on one side of the street, town, nation or even the world can have profound negative consequences for the other side. Everything in our world seems to be interconnected. Christians understand that everything in the created order has a purpose related to God and to every other created thing. And humanity has a special, God-given charge to oversee it all and serve as its custodian or gardener.

We must understand there is a similar balance in the family and how seemingly benign changes in the family have long consequences for the larger society. The changes we have seen in the family over the past thirty years have not been without consequence. Not one of them—widespread divorce, fatherlessness, bearing children out of wedlock, increasing cohabitation and untethered sexuality—has improved any important measure of human well-being.[1]

It's important for us to understand how making same-sex unions socially

---

[1]James Q. Wilson, *The Marriage Problem: How Our Culture Has Weakened Families* (New York: Harper Collins, 2002); Glenn T. Stanton, *Why Marriage Matters: Reasons to Believe in Marriage in Postmodern Society* (Colorado Springs: Pinon, 1997); Linda J. Waite and Maggie Gallagher,

equal to natural marriage can have similar unanticipated negative consequences.

QUESTION 1. *What if someone I know says he's a homosexual and he wants to marry his partner? How does that threaten my heterosexual marriage and family?*

ANSWER. If this were just about his family, then you might have a point. It may not have any substantial negative impact. But this public debate for same-sex marriage isn't just about a few different kinds of marriage here or there. It is about asking *every one* of us to radically change our own understanding of marriage forever.

If marriage were truly a private affair, which it is not, then same-sex marriage would have little impact on anyone's family. But marriage is just as much about the community as it is about the individuals, perhaps even more so. That's why marriages are public ceremonies, whether in churches or before civil authorities, and are regulated by laws. Marriage is a societal agreement.

No marriage is an island. Every marriage touches the community as a universally human community norm—a rule embraced by society for how we conduct ourselves sexually and domestically, and what we provide for children to meet their developmental needs. And every society must have a norm for what it expects and what it will *not* allow. Marriage is that social norm for the family. As humans, we are all connected and our decisions and actions—both public and private—*do* affect other people, even if it is indirect and not always evident. There are no truly private marriages.

Every healthy marriage proclaims to the community that men and women

---

The Case for Marriage: Why Married People are Happier, Healthier, and Better Off Financially (New York: Doubleday, 2000); David Popenoe, *Life Without Father: Compelling New Evidence That Fatherhood and Marriage Are Indispensable for the Good of Children and Society* (New York: Free Press, 1996); Katherine Reissman and Naomi Gerstel, "Marital Dissolution and Health: Do Males or Females Have Greater Risk?" *Social Science and Medicine* 20 (1985): 627-35; Edward O. Laumann et al., *The Social Organization of Sexuality: Sexual Practices in the United States* (Chicago: University of Chicago Press, 1994), p. 364 (table 10.5); Andrew Greeley, *Faithful Attraction: Discovering Intimacy, Love and Fidelity in American Marriage* (New York: Tom Doherty Association, 1991).

- need and complete each other in their differences
- should be faithful to one another sexually and emotionally
- have a duty to look out for each other's welfare
- share a commitment to bear and cooperatively raise the next generation

Marriage is also a statement to the community that men must commit themselves to one woman, to care for her as selflessly as he can, and support and care for the children that he sires with his wife. The decline of marriage over the past few decades has reduced the number of men who are helping women raise their children, creating widespread fatherlessness, one of our nation's most urgent social problems.[2] Same-sex marriage likely will contribute to this decline, even among heterosexual men. Won't lesbian families send the message to men that fathers are optional and lead men to increasingly see themselves that way? Gay male families tell us that a man committing himself to one woman is simply one lifestyle choice among many. So, men committing themselves to women will become increasingly optional. This is not good for men, and it won't be good for women or their children.

QUESTION 2. *How could same-sex marriage harm my children?*

ANSWER. Same-sex marriage teaches children and their generation that marriage is merely about fulfilling adult sexual and emotional desire, nothing more. Many approaches to and philosophies of heterosexual marriage already teach this, and same-sex marriage will only help solidify it.

Same-sex marriage—like easy divorce, cohabitation, pre- and extramarital sex, and unmarried childbearing—relativize family relationships. It promotes a smorgasbord mentality for family life: choose what suits your tastes, and one choice is as good as another. But no society has ever been able to sustain itself with such a view of family life.

Same-sex marriage will teach little boys that the idea of being a good family man—caring and sacrificing himself for one woman and their children—is not expected or even virtuous, but merely one lifestyle choice among

---

[2]David Blankenhorn, *Fatherless America: Confronting Our Most Urgent Social Problem* (New York: Basic Books, 1994).

many. Same-sex marriage teaches our daughters that being committed to and helping socialize a husband and bearing and raising children with him is also only one family lifestyle choice among many.

In short the entire meaning and significance of marriage itself, and what it means to be male and female, will be radically changed. So will the choices and behaviors of those who grow up within that altered social context.

QUESTION 3. *How does same-sex marriage harm our understanding of humanity?*

ANSWER. In some very profound and harmful ways.

Wife and *husband* become mere words we use to describe people in a relationship. They lose any vital meaning. In fact, marriage license clerks in Massachusetts have been instructed to start referring to people getting married as "Party A" and "Party B."[3] Thus the deep meaning of *husband* and *wife* are evacuated. With "Party A, you may now kiss Party B," our sons and daughters will miss the fact that men and women are uniquely completed and fulfilled when they love and commit to the "otherness" of male and female in marriage.

Mother and father become merely androgynous people engaged in the act of caring for kids. *Mother* and *father* become mere sentimental words used to address parents—not something special that men and women, as parents, *are*. Any apparent differences become merely superficial and of no practical consequence. In fact, saying children need mothers and fathers could become hate speech because it indicts same-sex families.

The terms *male* and *female* are emptied of significance. We exchange our appreciation of humanity, understood as the treasures of being male and female, for a "Mr. Potato Head" theory of humanity (same shell, interchangeable exterior parts!). The same-sex marriage proposition cannot tolerate any necessary, fundamental differences between the genders. If there were necessary differences, male and female would need each other and *every* same-

---

[3]Jonathan Finer, "Only Mass. Residents to Get Marriage Licenses," *The Washington Post*, April 30, 2004, p. A03; see also "Procedures to Perform (Solemnize) Marriages by Special One Day Designation," *Public Records Division*, William Francis Galvin, Secretary of the Commonwealth, accessed on June 15, 2004, at <www.sec.state.ma.us/pre/premar/marone.htm>.

sex family would be humanly incomplete. *Gender* in a society that accepts same-sex marriage can only refer to meaningless, impersonal, interchangeable parts. A socially equal—and not just tolerated—same-sex marriage does damage at a very fundamental level. In fact, *granting moral equality to even one same-sex marriage diminishes all of us at the very core of our humanity.*

The significance of gender is demolished by the essence of same-sex marriage. Once it is made morally equal to natural marriage it will diminish the femininity of every woman. There will be minimal differences of men and women left over, and they are purely physiological. A woman's surrogate womb becomes the only part of femininity that is needed to create a male same-sex family. A woman is reduced to a womb and its practical function, and this is a horrible message to send to women and girls. Reducing gender to physiology is, well, dehumanizing.

Similarly, one lesbian same-sex marriage—once it is seen as morally equal to natural marriage—will diminish the masculinity of every man, for the only thing important about manhood will be sperm. This is a bad message to send to men and boys. They are reduced to being impersonal parts—things, not persons. Both views are deeply antihuman because they are deeply anti-male and -female.

This turn in our understanding of gender will create far more—rather than less—confusion within us as individuals and dissension among us in our relationships with others; it will not allow us to be true to our respective genders—who we really are! Same-sex marriage deconstructs our humanity as expressed in our masculinity and femininity. Masculinity and femininity become morally, personally and interpersonally meaningless.

CONCLUSION

How could same-sex marriage hurt your family? First, we are not just talking about allowing one same-sex couple to marry. *All* of us are being asked to dramatically change our understanding of what marriage is, what the family does and how essential male and female are to both. Same-sex families—when not just merely tolerated but seen as socially equal to natural marriage and families—announce that the only inherent virtues male and female hold for the family are in their genetic, biological contributions to procreation: sperm, egg and womb. It is dehumanizing to reduce male and female to these impersonal dimensions because in deep and profound ways personhood, marriage and family is beautifully and intrinsically tied to gender. As we lose this, we lose an essential part to our humanity.

5

WOULDN'T GAY MARRIAGE MAKE
FOR A MORE OPEN AND EQUITABLE SOCIETY?

Christopher and Greg live across the street from Lauren and Adam. Lauren and Adam have four young children, two girls and two boys. Christopher has a son from his marriage to Lynn, which ended seven years ago when Christopher declared his feelings for Greg.

The two couples have been neighbors and friends for three years and they get along wonderfully. Greg and Adam ride their Harleys together most Sunday afternoons, while Christopher and Lauren share an interest in pottery, which they practice on the wheel in Christopher's garage studio. The couples alternate cookouts at each others' houses nearly every month in the spring and summer. Greg is teaching Lauren and Adam's children how to play the cello. These couples have a valuable friendship.

But one evening at one of their barbecues, Christopher and Greg's future plans came up. They spoke of wanting to go to another state that grants same-sex marriage licenses, get married and then return to Florida to sue in court for their marriage to be recognized in the "sunshine state." They would do this under the U.S. Constitution's full faith and credit clause, a provision that says things like drivers and wedding licenses issued in one state must be recognized by another state.

Christopher asked Adam and Lauren if they would allow their four-year-old daughter to be a ring bearer in the wedding along with his son. This was very uncomfortable for both Lauren and Adam. And Lauren was honest enough to let them know how uneasy they were about it. Greg got angry and asked why they couldn't accept his and Christopher's love. He apologized for his sharpness but pressed Lauren for an answer.

Adam stepped in and explained that while their regard for Christopher and Greg was genuine and obvious, and evidenced in their long and close friendship, they did have some strong feelings about what marriage is. Adam explained they were obviously able to tolerate Christopher and Greg's home life, but now they were being asked to do two things that conflicted. One was celebrating something that was important to their friends, which they desired to do, but the second was where the conflict lay. Adam and Lauren were being asked not just to tolerate something and accept their friends as friends but to betray their own understanding and conviction about what marriage and family is. Their four children would be receiving a different education about what marriage is by the sheer fact of their participation in a ceremony that would look the same but would be in essence something profoundly different. If they were to affirm a same-sex marriage, their own way of being married would be called into question in the eyes of their children. The meaning of their own family life would have to change if it were viewed as only one possible way of being married.

Adam and Lauren decided they couldn't participate in the ceremony, and while the two couples remain friends, their relationship isn't as strong as it was. Unfortunately, it was forever changed by Christopher's request and Greg's question. Christopher and Greg were not asking for mere acceptance; they already had that. With their request they were asking Lauren and Adam to change their own convictions about fundamental parts of their lives.

This scenario will work itself out in thousands of different ways in various work, family and neighbor relationships as same-sex marriages spread. Let's look at how to address the question of whether this will foster togetherness and understanding.

QUESTION 1. *Wouldn't accepting gay marriage help us all get along better?*

ANSWER. Actually, quite the opposite. It would alienate two key groups of people: (1) "married" gays from gays who don't want marriage and (2) couples like Greg and Christopher from much of the heterosexual community.

QUESTION 2. *How would same-sex marriage alienate homosexuals from each other?*

ANSWER. Same-sex marriage will create strong dissension in the homosexual community. It already has.

Judith Levine, a radical family deconstructionist, explains this in a recent article titled "Stop the Wedding: Why Gay Marriage Isn't Radical Enough." Levine says that marriage itself, gay *or* straight, is unfair because it alienates people. She says marriage "pushes the queerer queers of all persuasions—drag queens, club-crawlers, polyamorists, even ordinary single mothers or teenage lovers—further to the margins." She complains that marriage elevates marrying couples, be they gay or straight, and positions them as morally superior to other nonmarried couples, and this is unfair. As evidence of the fact she cites with disapproval some liberal clergy in Vermont who proclaim that married gays "exemplify a moral good that cannot be represented by so-called registered partnerships."[1] Same-sex marriage, she says, sets one part of the homosexual community, the more conservative and domestic "pro-marriage" crowd, against the more laissez-faire, "let's abolish *all* family categories and live how we want," crowd. Judith Levine is an advocate of this second group. There is a third group among homosexuals, those who say, "Marriage, why do we need it?"[2]

QUESTION 3. *How does same-sex marriage alienate heterosexuals from homosexuals?*

ANSWER. In ways very similar to the story of the two couples at the opening of this chapter. And scenarios like this will work themselves into thousands of good, meaningful relationships. Why? Because same-sex marriage asks heterosexuals to celebrate something most cannot believe in.[3] It's one thing

---

[1] Judith Levine, "Stop the Wedding! Why Gay Marriage Isn't Radical Enough," *The Village Voice*, July 23-29, 2003, <www.villagevoice.com/issues/0330/levine.php>.

[2] We explore the three "marriage attitude" groups in the homosexual community in greater detail in chap. 15.

[3] Polling numbers consistently show very strong public disapproval for the idea of same-sex marriage. See <www.marriagedebate.com/pdf/ssm_research.pdf>. Joshua K. Baker, "Summary of Opinion Research on Same-Sex Marriage," *iMAPP Policy Brief*, Institute for Marriage and Public Policy, December 5, 2003.

for a same-sex couple to live together like Greg and Christopher: they can live their lives, develop friendly relationships with their neighbors, and no one has to accept or reject their relationship. It's just what it is. But marriage is a different thing. A marriage is a call to the community to recognize and celebrate the relationship. That is why most people don't simply go to city hall. They have ceremonies and lavish receptions so that everyone can celebrate the union.

When a same-sex couple celebrates their marriage, they won't just ask their gay and lesbian friends to celebrate the new union, they will ask *all* those around them—friends, extended family, neighbors, coworkers—to celebrate also. Some will have no qualms about honoring this new kind of marriage. However, most will hesitate, for they won't be able to bless something they don't believe in.

These people will struggle, like Adam and Lauren, between their allegiance to their homosexual friends and their convictions about marriage and family. But they won't be able to ignore the wedding invitation. Because of the relationship and regard they have for the individual or couple, they will be forced to have a confrontation, hopefully a gracious one. Some will have to say, "I am sorry. We want to honor you as our friend, but we don't believe in marriage between members of the same sex. Therefore we can't honor your marriage." No doubt the relationship will suffer.

Imagine this basic dynamic played out in a thousand different family and friendship scenarios:

- Does a father pay for his daughter's lesbian wedding?
- Does the father walk her down the aisle?
- Do you attend the wedding shower?
- What about the baby showers that could follow?
- What kind of discussion develops when some coworkers want to share in buying a wedding present for their colleague and some don't? How will that work itself out civilly?
- Will in-laws really be able to celebrate the coming together of two families via the "marriage" of two guys or gals as they would with a husband and wife coming together?

These problems will arise because something that most of us believe is wrong is being forced on us. We will be divided between how we esteem our friends and how we esteem natural marriage. This will not bring us closer together but rather drive us further apart, as it did with Greg and Christopher and Adam and Lauren.

QUESTION 4. *Won't same-sex marriage take the emphasis off of gender differences and create a more gender-equitable society?*

ANSWER. Just the opposite. Marriage is one of the primary ways we get men and women to treat each other fairly.

If we adopt same-sex marriage as morally and socially equal to male-female marriage, then the qualities that make these relationships different—that one includes *both* male and female—become unnecessary. As we have pointed out earlier, male and female become unnecessary. The idea of a man curbing his passions, desires and aggression in order to care for his wife and children would no longer serve as a social ideal or expectation. But no society has ever, until the last several decades in developed Western cultures, accepted the idea that men don't necessarily need to do this. And the results have been disastrous in terms of increased child poverty (i.e., the feminization of poverty), declining educational attainment, diminished physical and mental health among children, and dramatic increases in physical and sexual abuse of both women and children.[4] A man committing himself exclusively to a woman and helping

---

[4]David Ellwood, *Poor Support: Poverty in the American Family* (New York: Basic Books, 1988); Ronald J. Angel and Jacqueline Worobey, "Single Motherhood and Children's Health," *Journal of Health and Social Behavior* 29 (1988): 38-52; Ronald J. Angel and Jacqueline L. Angel, *Painful Inheritance: Health and the New Generation of Fatherless Families* (Madison: University of Wisconsin Press, 1993); Deborah Dawson, "Family Structure and Children's Health and Well-Being: Data from the 1988 National Health Interview Survey on Child Health," *Journal of Marriage and the Family* 53 (1991): 573-84; Sara L. McLanahan, "Life Without Father: What Happens to Children?" Center for Research on Child Well-Being Working Paper 01-21 (Princeton, N.J.: Princeton University, 2001); Ronald P. Rohner and Robert A. Veneziano, "The Importance of Father Love: History and Contemporary Evidence," *Review of General Psychology* 5, no. 4 (2001): 382-405; Kyle D. Pruett, *Fatherneed: Why Father Care is as Essential as Mother Care for Your Child* (New York: Free Press, 2000); Michael Stiffman et al., "Household Composition and Risk of Fatal Child Maltreatment," *Pediatrics* 109 (2002): 615-21; Frank Putnam, "Ten Year Research Update Review: Child Sexual Abuse," *Journal of the American Academy of Child and Adolescent Psychiatry* 42 (2003): 269-79.

raise their children can't be offered as merely one "life choice" among many. And if we don't expect it as a society, men will not be inclined to do it.

As Rutgers sociologist David Popenoe warns, "In every society the main cultural institution designed for . . . enforcing high paternal investment . . . is marriage."[5] Margaret Mead found the same thing, indicating there is no known society where men will stay married very long unless they are required by the culture to do so.[6] As George Gilder has so eloquently pointed out, monogamous marriage is the only way societies transform men from cruising savages to good, faithful, family men. What is more, he explains, it is being married to a woman that socializes men.[7] No society has been able to show that men entering into close personal relationships with other men can accomplish this important social role. Marriage changes a man because he is married to a woman, someone who is his gender counterpart, not a mirror image of himself.

QUESTION 5. *Does a father's involvement in family life affect gender equality?*

ANSWER. Scott Coltrane, a sociologist at the University of California, looked at ninety different cultures to study how men's participation in child care related to the status of women in their culture. He found a very close connection, explaining, "Societies with significant paternal involvement in routine child care are more likely than father-absent societies to include women in public decisions and to allow women access to positions of authority."[8] And these involved fathers pass this greater respect for women on to the next generation via their influence on their sons. Noted gender psy-

---

[5]David Popenoe, *Life Without Father: Compelling New Evidence That Fatherhood and Marriage Are Indispensable for the Good of Children and Society* (New York: Free Press, 1996), p. 184.

[6]Margaret Mead, *Male and Female: A Study of the Sexes in a Changing World* (New York: William Morrow, 1949).

[7]George Gilder, *Men and Marriage* (Gretna, La.: Pelican, 1986). The same point is made by Gail Collins in her history of women in America, *America's Women: 400 Years of Dolls, Drudges, Helpmates and Heroines* (New York: William Morrow, 2003), pp. 3-8. She says one of the key, but underappreciated, roles women have played in American history is serving to make men behave and become productive citizens.

[8]Scott Coltrane, "Father-Child Relationships and the Status of Women: A Cross-Cultural Study," *American Journal of Sociology* 93 (1988): 1085. See also Scott Coltrane, "The Micropolitics of Gender in Nonindustrial Societies," *Gender and Society* 6 (1992): 86-107; Scott Coltrane, *Family Man: Fatherhood, Housework and Gender Equality* (New York: Oxford University Press, 1996).

chologist Mary Stewart Van Leeuwen explains, "when young boys have primary caretakers of both sexes, they are less likely as adults to engage in woman devaluing activities and in self-aggrandizing, cruel or overly competitive male cults."[9]

In addition, monogamy, which is necessary to temper sexual competitiveness in society, will get lost under same-sex marriage as well; monogamy in male homosexual relationships is difficult to sustain, even in long-term relationships.[10] And if we can't expect monogamy of homosexual males in marriage, the social-norms bar gets lowered for everyone, making it even more difficult to expect it of heterosexual males. We can be sure that because of human nature homosexual men, with their dismissal of a monogamous sexual ethic, will influence heterosexual men, not toward homosexuality but toward heterosexual infidelity. And this will happen much more than heterosexual men influencing homosexual men toward monogamy.[11] As a result, women will have a harder time finding faithful men, and it will become more difficult to defend themselves from the increasing number of sexually predatory males. Monogamy, as a social rule, keeps the sexual playing field more level and safer for women. A change in that field isn't (and *hasn't* been) good news for women.

Women will suffer in another important way. It's not illogical to consider

---

[9]Mary Stewart Van Leeuwen, *My Brother's Keeper: What the Social Sciences Do (and Don't) Tell Us About Masculinity* (Downers Grove, Ill.: InterVarsity Press, 2002), p. 121.

[10]Maria Xiridou et al., "The Contributions of Steady and Casual Partnerships to the Incidence of HIV Infection Among Homosexual Men in Amsterdam," *AIDS* 17 (2003): 1029-38; David Demo et al., eds., *Handbook on Family Diversity* (New York: Oxford University Press, 2000), p. 73; David McWhirter and Andrew Mattison found that in their study of 156 homosexual males in relationships ranging from one to thirty-seven years, only seven couples have a totally monogamous relationship, and each of these men had only been together less than five years. See David McWhirter and Andrew Mattison, *The Male Couple: How Relationships Develop* (Englewood Cliffs, N.J.: Prentice Hall, 1984), pp. 252-53.

[11]In a famous essay Daniel Patrick Moynihan discusses this sociological phenomenon of lowering community standards and how that accepted lower standard for small populations negatively influences the larger population, which would not normally participate in such behavior. And such a lowering of standards seduces us all "to just learn to live with it," as Moynihan says. But no society can just live with a plummeting standard of monogamy. See Daniel Patrick Moynihan, "Defining Deviancy Down," *The American Scholar* 62 (1993): 17-30.

that same-sex marriage could open a door for polygamy and possibly group marriage. How? Because as we have seen, if same-sex marriage advocates can successfully argue in court that marriage shouldn't necessarily be about *men* and *women*—as they have done—why shouldn't multiple-partner marriage advocates (for whom there are many, and they are sincere) be able to successfully argue that marriage shouldn't be about *number of partners*. Wouldn't it be unjust to allow one redefinition of marriage (regarding gender) without allowing the other (regarding number)?

In polygamous cultures men collect women as wives, either in groups or in one relationship after another. A polygamous world is a man's world. Polyandry (one woman, multiple husbands) is only found in 0.5 percent of all human societies.[12] Monogamous marriage is democracy for the domestic and sexual lives of men and women. Any move away from this tips the sexual playing field to men's advantage—and women lose.

QUESTION 6. *But wasn't polygamy practiced in the Bible?*

ANSWER. Yes, but not everything we find written in the Bible establishes a "biblical" standard. Judas betrayed Christ, his friend, but just because we find his betrayal in the Bible doesn't mean we should betray our friends. Sometimes the Bible serves as a historical record, telling us what happened, and other times it's a guidebook, instructing us on how to live godly, Christlike lives. We study and pray, asking God to help us discern the difference.

But what kind of marriage does Scripture promote and bless? We will address this more in the conclusion of this book, but we will give a thumbnail picture here.

Soon after God created Adam, God said something very important about Adam, something very profound and foundational about all of humanity. He looked at Adam standing in the Garden, fresh from the creative hand of God, and declared, "It is not good for the man to be alone" (Genesis 2:18). This is the only part of creation that God declared "not good." In fact, Adam had perfect communion with God (remember, this was before the Fall), and God

---

[12]Helen E. Fisher, *Anatomy of Love: The Natural History of Monogamy, Adultery and Divorce* (New York: W. W. Norton, 1992), p. 69.

said this was not good enough for Adam. Adam was not made to live by himself or with God alone. He was made for another. Jews, Christians and Muslims, unlike secular humanists, understand that people need God *and* people. Unlike the hyperspiritual religionists, they understand we need more than God. People need God *and* other people. This is because of the way God created us.

So what is God's answer? It is Eve, a woman. God gave Adam exactly what he needed and Eve exactly what she needed. He didn't give Adam a number of wives, just one. And he blessed Adam and Eve and told them they would become one flesh (Genesis 2:24). Jesus reiterates and affirms this in Matthew 19:4-6. Multiple spouses can't become one flesh. It's God's ideal that we all have one spouse and the two—husband and wife—will become one flesh in marriage.

CONCLUSION

Gay marriage would not bring our society closer together. It would drive us further apart. It would further alienate homosexuals and heterosexuals by forcing heterosexuals to accept something that most can't accept. What is more, it would alienate the more conservative homosexuals from the more radical ones, those who reject sexual norms and see this rejection as the defining virtue of homosexuality. It would also hurt women and children by further compromising the virtue of monogamy and the fact that a good, faithful family man who devotes himself to his wife and children is a positive social norm.

6

DON'T CHILDREN JUST NEED
LOVING PARENTS?

We were engaged in a public debate on the wisdom of the same-sex family in a packed meeting room on a university campus. We were making the case that it is never compassionate to intentionally form families in which children will deliberately be denied either their mother or their father. A couple, two women, stood up at the start of the question-and-answer part of the program and asked, "How in the world can you say that we cannot be loving parents? We have two sons at home, and they get all the love children in any heterosexual home receive. Perhaps even more!" The crowd roared in approval. How could we say these parents weren't loving?

Well, we said nothing of the sort. We had no reason to doubt that these two nice women love the children they are raising and that these children benefit from their love. Neither do we doubt that most parents in same-sex homes love the children they are raising.

But didn't our society say something very similar at the dawn of the failed divorce revolution? It didn't matter if mom and dad still lived together, because their children would still have two parents who love them dearly, even if from a distance. In fact, our children still hear that regularly in a little ditty sung by the kids on *Barney & Friends* about their parents living far from them but still loving them every day.

These parents may love their children every day, from a distance, but what we have learned from our nation's long divorce experiment is that children need their *mom* and *dad* to love them every day right there in the home.[1] We told the two women in the debate that evening that, oddly enough, a parent's ability to love is not the most important thing for children's well-being. For scholars have come to see that the mitigating love of the parents could not erase the harmful impact that divorce wrought in the lives of children because these children didn't have their mothers *and* fathers involved in the daily routine of life. And the fact that the biological parent is replaced by a loving stepparent does little to make the problems better. In many important ways, it makes them worse, and a convincing wealth of social science, medical and psychological data reveals this.[2] Likewise, how can we assume the love of two women or two men will be able to erase the harm to children by being raised apart from their mother and father? We can't.[3]

QUESTION 1. *Why aren't loving parents enough for children?*

ANSWER. It seems the Beatles got it wrong! You need a whole lot more than love when it comes to raising healthy, well-adjusted children.

---

[1]E. Mavis Hetherington, *For Better or For Worse: Divorce Reconsidered* (New York: W. W. Norton, 2002); Judith Wallerstein et al., *The Unexpected Legacy of Divorce: A 25 Year Landmark Study* (New York: Hyperion, 2000); Judith Wallerstein, "The Long-Term Effects of Divorce on Children: A Review," *Journal of the American Academy of Child and Adolescent Psychiatry* 30 (1991): 349-60.

[2]David Popenoe, "The Evolution of Marriage and the Problems of Stepfamilies: A Biosocial Perspective," in *Stepfamilies: Who Benefits? Who Does Not?* ed. Alan Booth and Judy Dunn (Hillsdale, N.J.: Lawrence Erlbaum, 1994); Nicholas Zill, "Understanding Why Children in Stepfamilies Have More Learning and Behavior Problems Than Children in Nuclear Families," in Alan Booth and Judy Dunn, eds., *Stepfamilies: Who Benefits? Who Does Not?* (Hillsdale, N.J.: Lawrence Erlbaum, 1994), p. 98; Martin Daly and Margo Wilson, "Child Abuse and Other Risks of Not Living with Both Parents," *Ethology and Sociobiology* 6 (1985): 197-210; Martin Daly and Margo Wilson, *Homicide* (New York: Aldine de Gruyter, 1988), p. 87-88; Margo Wilson and Martin Daly, "Risk of Maltreatment of Children Living With Stepparents," in *Child Abuse and Neglect: Biosocial Dimensions*, ed. R. Gelles and J. Lancaster (New York: Aldine de Gruyter, 1987), p. 230; Michael Stiffman et al., "Household Composition and Risk of Fatal Child Maltreatment," *Pediatrics* 109 (2002): 615-21; "Shuttle Diplomacy," *Psychology Today*, July-August 1993, p. 15; Douglas B. Downey, "Understanding Academic Achievement Among Children in Stephouseholds: The Role of Parental Resources, Sex of Stepparent and Sex of Child," *Social Forces* 73 (1995): 875-94; William L. MacDonald and Alfred DeMaris, "Parenting Stepchildren and Biological Children: The Effect of Stepparent's Gender and New Biological Children," *Journal of Family Issues* 17 (1996): 5-25.

[3]We will address this more fully in chaps. 7-8.

Kids need their mother *and* father. The majority of children growing up in same-sex homes are being raised by lesbians—intentionally fatherless homes.[4] While our hearts tell us that children need their mothers, thousands of social-science studies tell us that children suffer in all the important ways when they live in a home without their father.[5] And having an additional new parent replacing the father does little to make things better.[6] While a compassionate and caring society *always* comes to the aid of motherless and father-

[4]Tavia Simmons and Martin O'Connell, "Married-Couple and Unmarried-Partner Households: 2000," *U.S. Census 2000*, Census 2000 Special Reports, February 2003, p. 10.

[5]Ronald P. Rohner and Robert A. Veneziano, "The Importance of Father Love: History and Contemporary Evidence," *Review of General Psychology* 5, no. 4 (2001): 382-405; David Popenoe, *Life Without Father: Compelling Evidence That Fatherhood and Marriage Are Indispensable for the Good of Children* (New York: Free Press, 1996); Glenn T. Stanton, *Why Marriage Matters: Reasons to Believe in Marriage in Postmodern Society* (Colorado Springs: Pinon, 1997); Kyle D. Pruett, *Fatherneed: Why Father Care Is as Essential as Mother Care for Your Child* (New York: Free Press, 2000); David Blankenhorn, *Fatherless America: Confronting Our Most Urgent Social Problem* (New York: Basic Books, 1994); Sara McLanahan and Gary Sandefur, *Growing Up with a Single Parent: What Hurts, What Helps* (Cambridge, Mass.: Harvard University Press, 1994); Ellen Bing, "The Effect of Child-Rearing Practices on the Development of Differential Cognitive Abilities," *Child Development* 34 (1963): 631-48; Deborah Dawson, "Family Structure and Children's Health and Well-Being: Data from the 1988 National Health Interview Survey on Child Health," *Journal of Marriage and the Family* 53 (1991): 573-84; Scott Coltrane, "Father-Child Relationships and the Status of Women: A Cross-Cultural Study," *American Journal of Sociology* 93 (1988): 1088; Michael Gottfredson and Travis Hirschi, *A General Theory of Crime* (Stanford, Calif.: Stanford University Press, 1990), p. 103; Richard Koestner et al., "The Family Origins of Empathic Concern: A Twenty-Six Year Longitudinal Study," *Journal of Personality and Social Psychology* 58 (1990): 709-17; E. Mavis Hetherington, "Effects of Father Absence on Personality Development in Adolescent Daughters," *Developmental Psychology* 7 (1972): 313-26; Irwin Garfinkel and Sara McLanahan, *Single Mothers and Their Children: A New American Dilemma* (Washington, D.C.: Urban Institute Press, 1986), pp. 30-31; Sara L. McLanahan, "Life Without Father: What Happens to Children?" Center for Research on Child Wellbeing Working Paper 01-21 (Princeton, N.J.: Princeton University, 2001); Paul R. Amato and Fernando Rivera, "Paternal Involvement and Children's Behavior Problems," *Journal of Marriage and the Family* 61 (1999): 375-84; David Ellwood, *Poor Support: Poverty in the American Family* (New York: Basic Books, 1988), p. 46; Ronald J. Angel and Jacqueline Worobey, "Single Motherhood and Children's Health," *Journal of Health and Social Behavior* 29 (1988): 38-52; Richard Koestner et al., "The Family Origins of Empathic Concern: A Twenty-Six Year Longitudinal Study," *Journal of Personality and Social Psychology* 58 (1990): 709-17; L. Remez, "Children Who Don't Live with Both Parents Face Behavioral Problems," *Family Planning Perspectives*, January-February 1992; Wallerstein et al., *Unexpected Legacy*; Nicholas Zill, Donna Morrison and Mary Jo Coiro, "Long-Term Effects of Parental Divorce on Parent-Child Relationships, Adjustment, and Achievement in Young Adulthood," *Journal of Family Psychology* 7 (1993): 91-103.

[6]See citations for increased problems in stepfamilies in note 2 above.

less families, a wise and loving society *never* intentionally creates fatherless or motherless families. But that is exactly what every same-sex family does and for no other reason than adults desire such families. No child-development theory says children *need* parents of the same gender—as loving as they might be—but rather that children *need* their mother and father.

The two most loving mothers in the world can't be a father to a little boy. Love can't equip mothers to teach a little boy how to be a man. Likewise, the two most loving men can't be a mother to a child. Love does little to help a man teach a little girl how to be a woman. Can you imagine two men guiding a young girl through her first menstrual cycle or helping her through the awkwardness of picking out her first bra? Such a situation might make for a funny television sitcom but not a very good real-life situation for a young girl.

Here are some questions to think about. How can two loving, homosexual men teach a young boy to care for and love a woman? How will the boy observe this in a home where it doesn't exist? What will two loving moms teach a little girl about men? How healthy will that picture be? Don't same-sex relationships, by definition, fail to provide many of the important things children need, since they are missing one of that child's natural parents and one essential part of humanity?

Dr. Merilee Clunis and Dr. Dorsey Green know quite a bit about lesbian parenting. In *The Lesbian Parenting Book* they admit that the same-sex parenting proposition is subjecting children to a massive, unproven social experiment. They write: "It will be interesting to see over time whether lesbian sons have an easier or harder time developing their gender identity than do boys with live-in fathers."[7] *It will be interesting to see?* When we are talking about the development of children, we can't simply hope it will all work out. We have to *know* how it will turn out. Children are not laboratory rats.

But recent research indicates it won't work out well. A major study published in the prestigious *American Sociological Review,* conducted by research-

---

[7]D. Merilee Clunis and G. Dorsey Green, *The Lesbian Parenting Book: A Guide to Creating Families and Raising Kids,* 2nd ed. (New York: Seal Press, 2003), p. 243.

ers who are politically sympathetic to the same-sex family, found that 64 percent of young adults raised by lesbian mothers considered having same-sex erotic relationships either in the past, now or in the future. Only 17 percent of young adults in heterosexual families reported the same thing.[8] What is more, this study reports that heterosexual mothers were significantly more likely to desire that their boys engage in masculine activities and their daughters in feminine ones, while "lesbian mothers had no such interest. Their preference for their child's play was gender-neutral."[9]

James Q. Wilson, one of the world's brightest and most well-respected sociologists, recently wrote a very important article on the importance of marriage. There, he says:

> Almost everyone—a few retrograde scholars excepted—agrees that children in mother-only homes suffer harmful consequences: the best studies show that these youngsters are more likely than those in [mother-father] families to be suspended from school, have emotional problems, become delinquent, suffer from abuse and take drugs.

He explains that some of the difference in these children, perhaps half, can be explained by the economic difference of living without a father. But, he explains, "the rest of the difference is explained by a mother living without a husband."[10]

While Professor Wilson is referring primarily to heterosexual men leaving their families, or mothers bearing children without husbands, there is good reason to believe that these problems in child development can't be softened if a mother merely lived with a wife instead of the father of her children.

QUESTION 2. *Do we really know what happens to kids raised without a father?*

ANSWER. Clunis and Green, in their lesbian handbook, are wrong. We

---

[8]Judith Stacey and Timothy Biblarz, "(How) Does the Sexual Orientation of Parents Matter?" *American Sociological Review* 66 (2001): 170-71.

[9]Ibid., p. 172.

[10]James Q. Wilson, "Why We Don't Marry," *City Journal*, Winter 2002, <www.city-journal.org/html/12_1_why_we.html>.

know what happens to children who are raised without fathers. There is no doubt, for it is documented in not tens or hundreds but in thousands of published academic studies over the past decades. In fact, seldom have the social, psychological and medical sciences come to a more sure conclusion than in how children need a mother and a father.

1. *General contributions dads make to healthy child development.* In a 1999 review of the past twenty years' studies examining how fathers contribute to child development, it is explained that 82 percent of these studies found "significant associations between positive father involvement and offspring well-being."[11]

In an analysis of over one hundred studies on parent-child relationships, it was found that having a loving and nurturing father was *as important* for a child's happiness, well-being, and social and academic success *as having a loving and nurturing mother.* Some studies indicated father love was a *stronger* contributor than mother love to some important positive child well-being outcomes. The study concludes: "Overall, father love appears to be as heavily implicated as mother love in offsprings' psychological well-being and health."[12]

2. *Dads grow security, confidence and attachment.* Infants feel more secure and are more likely to explore the world around them with increased enthusiasm and curiosity when they have an active father in their lives from the first eighteen to twenty-four months of life. This is because fathers are more active in play and slower to help the child through frustrating situations than are mothers. Fathers are more likely than women to promote problem-solving competencies and independence in the child.[13]

3. *Dads increase school readiness and behavior.* Children who have an involved father in their lives in the early years show up for school with more of the character qualities needed for learning. They are more patient, curious

---

[11]Paul R. Amato and Fernando Rivera, "Paternal Involvement and Children's Behavior Problems," *Journal of Marriage and the Family* 61 (1999): 375-84.

[12]Ronald P. Rohner and Robert A. Veneziano, "The Importance of Father Love: History and Contemporary Evidence," *Review of General Psychology* 5, no. 4 (2001): 382-405.

[13]Pruett, *Fatherneed,* pp. 41-42.

and confident. They are more capable of remaining in their seats, waiting patiently for their teacher and maintaining interest in their own work.[14]

Dr. Kyle Pruett from Yale Medical School has spent much of his career researching how father love is as essential as mother love. His book *Fatherneed* reports on a major scientific study that found kids with fathers had

- lowered levels of disruptive behavior, acting out, depression and telling lies
- higher levels of obeying parents, being kind to others and being responsible
- fewer general behavioral problems

Pruett also found that girls with fathers were happier, more confident and willing to try new things compared to girls without fathers. He concludes, "positive father care is associated with more pro-social, and positive moral behavior overall in boys and girls."[15]

If we want more children with these qualities, we have to advocate that as many children as possible grow up with their fathers. Same-sex families move us in the opposite direction.

4. *Dads contribute to stronger cognitive, motor and verbal development.* Psychologist Ellen Bing was one of the first scholars to explore how fatherhood affects child well-being. In the early 1960s she found that children who had fathers who read to them regularly were more likely to do much better in many important cognitive skill categories than children who didn't have fathers who read to them. One of the strongest benefits was a substantial increase in a daughter's verbal skills. Interestingly, mother-reading time did not strongly affect verbal skill development in daughters or sons. Only father-reading time did.[16]

A study nearly ten years later published in *Developmental Psychology* found that both well-fathered preschool boys and girls had increased verbal

---

[14]Henry B. Biller, *Father and Families: Paternal Factors in Child Development* (Westport, Conn.: Auburn House, 1993).

[15]Pruett, *Fatherneed*, p. 52.

[16]Ellen Bing, "The Effect of Child-Rearing Practices on the Development of Differential Cognitive Abilities," *Child Development* 34 (1963): 631-48.

skills compared with kids with either absent or overbearing fathers.[17]

Professor Henry Biller, noted fatherhood researcher, time and again finds that father-involved children are more confident and successful in solving complex mathematical and logical puzzles. This is because fathers tend to be more specialized in and have a higher interest for analytical problems. Norma Radin found that high levels of father involvement contributed to higher mathematical competencies in young daughters.[18]

Dr. Michael Yogman conducted a study published in a major child psychiatry journal on the role fathers play in overcoming the effects of premature birth in Latino, African American and other inner-city populations. Yogman found these preemies with highly involved fathers had substantially higher cognitive skills than those children who didn't have involved fathers at three years of age.[19]

5. *Dads help kids make wise life choices.* Research from the University of Pennsylvania found that children who feel a closeness and warmth with their father are twice as likely to enter college, 75 percent less likely to have a child in their teen years, 80 percent less likely to be incarcerated and half as likely to show various signs of depression.[20]

Dr. Barbara Dafoe Whitehead explains that a white teenage girl from an advantaged background is five times more likely to become a teen mother if she grows up in a home without both of her biological parents.[21] This is because young girls who know the love, tenderness and respect of a father are not as likely to seek the attention and approval of young boys. Their confi-

---

[17]Norma Radin, "Father-Child Interaction and the Intellectual Functioning of Four-Year-Old Boys," *Developmental Psychology* 6 (1972): 353-61.

[18]Henry B. Biller, "The Father and Personality Development: Paternal Deprivation and Sex-Role Development," in *The Role of the Father in Child Development*, ed. Michael E. Lamb (New York: Wiley, 1981), p. 104; Norma Radin, cited in Pruett, *Fatherneed*, p. 45.

[19]Michael Yogman et al., "Father Involvement and Cognitive/Behavioral Outcomes of Preterm Infants," *Journal of the American Academy of Child and Adolescent Psychiatry* 34 (1995): 58-66.

[20]Frank Furstenberg and Kathleen Harris, "When and Why Fathers Matter: Impacts of Father Involvement on Children of Adolescent Mothers," in *Young Unwed Fathers: Changing Roles and Emerging Policies*, ed. R. Lerman and T. Ooms (Philadelphia: Temple University Press, 1993).

[21]Barbara Dafoe Whitehead, "Facing the Challenge of Fragmented Families," *The Philanthropy Roundtable* 9.1 (1995): 21.

dence around men keeps them from being manipulated by the sexual pressures of opportunistic boys. Besides, fathers on the family scene are more likely to protect their daughters from such boys.

The likelihood that a young male will engage in criminal activity *doubles* if he is raised without a father and *triples* if he lives in a neighborhood with a high concentration of fatherless families.[22]

6. *Dads help curb violence in boys.* If there is no significant male in the young man's life to teach him how to display his masculinity in socially acceptable ways, he will demand that the community recognize his strength and masculinity by engaging in violence, intimidation and tomcatting. This is why gang activity is much higher in communities with low concentrations of involved fathers. A boy with a father who regularly tells him he has what it takes to succeed in society is not likely to feel the need to prove it to others through violence and sexual aggressiveness. You don't find well-fathered boys in gangs.

In "Juvenile Homicide in America," Kathleen Heide says, "Boys need [male] role models to define themselves as males. When fathers are absent, young males are more likely to exaggerate their purported masculinity."[23] And forensic psychologist Shawn Johnston notes, "The research is absolutely clear, . . . the one human being most capable of curbing the antisocial aggression of a boy is his biological father."[24] Could lesbian homes increase violence and gang activity among young boys? Research is clear that it could because they deny a boy his father!

7. *Dads help kids develop empathy and compassion.* While fathers help young boys become less violent, they also help children become more compassionate and caring. A long-term study started in the 1950s found that the strongest indicator for a child being empathic later in adulthood was warm

---

[22]Anne Hill and June O'Neil, *Underclass Behaviors in the United States: Measurements and Analysis or Determinants* (New York: City University of New York, 1993).

[23]Kathleen Heide, "Juvenile Homicide in America: How Can We Stop the Killing?," *Behavioral Sciences and the Law* 15 (1997): 203-20.

[24]Shawn Johnston, quoted in *The Pittsburgh Tribune Review*, March 29, 1998, from Wade F. Horn and Tom Sylvester, *Father Facts*, 4th ed. (Gaithersburg, Md.: National Fatherhood Initiative, 2002), p. 106.

father involvement in the early years of the child's life.[25]

Another twenty-six-year-long study found that the number one factor in developing empathy in children was father involvement. Fathers spending regular time alone with their children translated into children who became compassionate adults.[26]

8. Dads encourage gender equity. As noted earlier, Scott Coltrane and Mary Stewart Van Leeuwen found a very close connection between fathers being highly involved in their sons' lives and gender equality (see page 65). These involved fathers pass on this greater respect for women to the next generation via their influence on their sons. In contrast, boys raised in fatherless homes will be less likely to pass on an essential respect for women to the next generation.

The research is very clear. We know fathers matter, and they matter in deep and, at times, unsuspected ways. Leading child psychologist Michael E. Lamb reminds us that fathers have become the "forgotten contributors to child development."[27]

Dr. David Popenoe, a leading family sociologist from Rutgers University explains:

> Fathers are far more than just "second adults" in the home. They provide protection and economic support and male role models. They have a parenting style that is *significantly different from that of mother and that difference is important in healthy child development.*[28]

Our hearts tell us that all children need their mothers. The social sciences clearly show us that children also need their fathers. It is unsound to think that a father can be replaced by a loving woman or a mother by a loving man. To say so flies in the face of a wealth of research, and it would mean that mothers and fathers are *optional* in the life of a child. Can anyone honestly believe this?

---

[25]Robert R. Sears et al., *Patterns of Childrearing* (Evanston, Ill.: Row Peterson, 1957); see also Pruett, *Fatherneed,* p. 48.

[26]Richard Koestner et al., "The Family Origins of Empathic Concern: A Twenty-Six Year Longitudinal Study," *Journal of Personality and Social Psychology* 58 (1990): 709-17.

[27]Michael E. Lamb, "Fathers: The Forgotten Contributors to Child Development," *Human Development* 18 (1975): 245-66.

[28]Popenoe, *Life Without Father,* p. 163 (emphasis added).

CONCLUSION

Same-sex homes deny children of either a biological mother or father. And research on the importance of biological fathers will not allow us to cast off fathers so easily if we care about healthy child development. Dr. Kyle Pruett, after reviewing the large body of research on father involvement and child development, concludes that "these findings take us beyond a shadow of a doubt here" that fathers play an important and irreplaceable role in healthy child development. He adds, "the closer the connection between father and child, the better off they both are now and in the future."[29]

---

[29]Pruett, *Fatherneed,* pp. 44, 41. We will discuss more on how children benefit from a married mother and father in chaps. 9-10.

7

HAVEN'T PROFESSIONAL MEDICAL GROUPS SAID SAME-SEX PARENTING IS FINE FOR KIDS?

Jackie was asking her pediatrician about an article she saw in the newspaper a week earlier. One of the major pediatric medical associations had announced its determination that children who are raised by two men or two women are very similar to children who grow up with a mother and a father. The doctor confirmed that this was the case, which perplexed Jackie. She wondered how her or her husband mattered to the parenting process if two men or two women could do the job just as well. She knew that she was a different kind of parent from her husband, and not just because of personality but because she was a woman. She knew her husband was a different kind of parent because he was a man. She knew that her five children benefited from this difference. She observed it on a regular basis. She asked her pediatrician about what she was thinking. Was she off base? Was she missing something?

The doctor answered that she agreed with Jackie. She observed it in her practice every week: the way fathers interacted with their children and how that contrasted with the way mothers did. She knew mothers and fathers mattered. Jackie then asked how she could be at odds with her medical association. The pediatrician laughed, surprised at Jackie's naiveté. "Many of these types of statements from these professional organizations are mostly politically motivated and not driven by good science." "Many of my colleagues," she continued, "have organized and written strong letters of protest to this statement. We were never asked our opinion." Jackie was not surprised. As little as she knew about healthy development theories, she knew her own children and those of her friends and family. She knew both mothers and fathers mattered.

QUESTION 1. *What about the statement by the American Academy of Pediatrics? Didn't they find in their research that there was no real difference in kids raised by same-sex or different-sex parents?*

ANSWER. Yes, that is what they said. The American Academy of Pediatrics (AAP) announced in early February 2002 in a "Technical Report" that "a growing body of scientific literature demonstrates that children who grow up with 1 or 2 gay or lesbian parents fare as well in emotional, cognitive, social, and sexual functioning as do children whose parents are heterosexual."[1] However, there are many reasons, beyond all the research we just looked at in the previous chapter, to be suspicious about the conclusion of the AAP's report.

QUESTION 2. *How did the AAP come to this conclusion?*

ANSWER. It wasn't by all the learned pediatricians carefully examining all the available research and collectively concluding same-sex parenting was just fine. The "Technical Report" came from a small, eight-member committee within the AAP, and not the larger membership. In fact, this report brought the strongest negative reaction the AAP has ever received from its membership on any issue. An e-mail memo from the lead author of this report on same-sex parenting to a small group of members in the Academy is very telling . . .

> The AAP has received more messages—almost all of them CRITICAL—from members about the recent Policy Statement on coparent [same-sex] adoption than it has EVER received on any other topic. . . . This is a serious problem, as it means that it will become harder to continue the work we have been doing *to use the AAP as a vehicle for positive change.*[2]

If the lead author is more concerned about how the AAP can be *used* as a vehicle for change, we have to ask whether this organization is more con-

---

[1]Ellen C. Perrin, "Technical Report: Coparent and Second-Parent Adoption by Same-Sex Parents," *Pediatrics* 109, no. 2 (2002): 341.

[2]E-mail memo from Ellen Perrin, M.D., to select AAP members, dated February 15, 2002 (emphasis added).

cerned with serious science and the health of children or with social engineering and activism.

QUESTION 3. *But couldn't this committee have dealt fairly with the current research on same-sex parenting?*

ANSWER. Dr. Ellen Perrin, the lead author of the AAP's "Technical Report," is also coauthor of a 1994 study published in *Pediatrics in Review* titled "Children of Gay and Lesbian Parents." That study explained: "Unfortunately, the research (examining kids in same-sex parenting homes) to date has limitations, including small sample size, non-random subject selection, narrow range of socioeconomic and racial background, and lack of long-term longitudinal follow-up."[3]

Perrin's AAP "Technical Report," published eight years later, cautioned similar reservations, "The small and nonrepresentative samples studied and the relatively young age of most of the children suggest some reserve." This more recent report recognized why these methodological limitations exist, "Research exploring the diversity of parental relationships among gay and lesbian parents *is just beginning.*"[4] But these original and persisting methodological problems, rooted in a lack of good, sound research, did not prevent the AAP from making a strong conclusion. Within sentences of the two previously stated cautions, the Academy claims "the weight of evidence gathered during several decades using diverse samples and methodologies is persuasive in demonstrating that there is no systematic difference between gay and non-gay parents" in parenting outcomes.[5]

We find it interesting that a study claiming the research is still in its infancy can at the same time draw such a strong and "persuasive" conclusion from that small and immature research.

QUESTION 4. *How could they say that, in terms of outcomes, children*

---

[3]M. A. Gold, E. Perrin, D. Futterman, S. B. Friedman, "Children of Gay or Lesbian Parents," *Pediatrics in Review* 15 (1994): 354-58.
[4]Perrin, "Technical Report," p. 343 (emphasis added).
[5]Ibid.

raised in heterosexual homes look pretty much like children raised in ho-
mosexual homes?

ANSWER. First, this small committee of activists apparently wanted to say
this so people would think this new family experiment was all right for children. Second, they qualified their findings in the report in subtle ways. Let
us explain.

There are many kinds of heterosexual parenting situations. Some do very
well at raising healthy kids. Some do a poorer job. What is the AAP comparing same-sex parenting to?

The AAP "Technical Report" quickly explains what kind of heterosexual
homes they are comparing same-sex homes to: "these [same-sex] families
closely resemble stepfamilies formed after heterosexual couples divorce."[6]
The report also says that most children in homosexual and lesbian families
come to that family via the divorce of their original heterosexual family.
Given this, the report indicates, "the considerable research literature that has
accumulated addressing this issue has generally revealed that children of divorced lesbian mothers grow up in ways very similar to children of divorced
heterosexual mothers."[7]

This raises the questions, How healthy are heterosexual step- and divorced families, and are they similar to intact, heterosexual families in providing good things for children? Is intentionally creating more of these kinds
of families good for children? There is strong research to indicate that the
AAP's conclusion gives little comfort to those concerned about child well-
being. Consider the following:

1. Research on children in stepfamilies. David Popenoe observes:

> Social scientists used to believe that, for positive child outcomes, step-
> families were preferable to single-parent families. Today, we are not so
> sure. Stepfamilies typically have an economic advantage, but some re-
> cent studies indicate that the children of stepfamilies have as many be-
> havioral and emotional problems as the children of single-parent

---

[6]Ibid., p. 341.
[7]Ibid., p. 342.

families, and possibly more. . . . Stepfamily problems, in short, may be so intractable that *the best strategy for dealing with them is to do everything possible to minimize their occurrence.*[8]

A common finding is that stepparents provide less warmth and communicate less with their children than do biological parents.[9]

Children from stepfamilies, where their biological father is missing, are eighty times more likely to have to repeat a grade in school and twice as likely to be expelled or suspended, when compared to children living with both biological parents.[10] Children living in stepfamilies are also likely to have significantly greater "emotional, behavioral, and academic problems" than children living with their biological mother and father.[11]

There are significantly higher degrees of emotional and behavioral problems, needs for psychological help, and reports of poor general health (along with a greater likelihood of depression) and self-esteem for children in stepfamilies compared to their peers in biological parented homes.[12] Adolescents in stepfamilies, according to a 1998 study, experience significantly higher rates of frequent drug use in grades eight through ten than did children living with their mother and father.[13]

Research on child abuse indicates that preschool children who live with one biological parent and one stepparent are forty times more likely to become a victim of abuse than children living with a biological mother and fa-

---

[8]David Popenoe, "The Evolution of Marriage and the Problems of Stepfamilies: A Biosocial Perspective," in *Stepfamilies: Who Benefits? Who Does Not?* ed. Alan Booth and Judy Dunn (Hillsdale, N.J.: Lawrence Erlbaum, 1994), pp. 5, 19 (emphasis added).

[9]E. Thomson, S. McLanahan, and R. Curtin, "Family Structure, Gender, and Parental Socialization," *Journal of Marriage and the Family* 54 (1992): 368-78.

[10]Nicholas Zill, "Understanding Why Children in Stepfamilies Have More Learning and Behavior Problems Than Children in Nuclear Families," in *Stepfamilies: Who Benefits? Who Does Not?* ed. Alan Booth and Judy Dunn (Hillsdale, N.J.: Lawrence Erlbaum, 1994), p. 100.

[11]Ibid., p. 98.

[12]Bonnie Barber and Janice Lyons, "Family Process and Adolescent Adjustment in Intact and Remarried Families," *Journal of Youth and Adolescence* 23 (1994): 421-36; see also Popenoe, "Evolution of Marriage," p. 5.

[13]Jeanne Jenkins and Sabrina Zunguze, "The Relationship of Family Structure to Adolescent Drug Use, Peer Affiliation, and Perception of Peer Acceptance of Drug Use," *Adolescence* 33 (1998): 811-22.

ther.[14] Findings such as this led domestic-violence researchers Martin Daly and Margo Wilson to conclude, "stepparenthood per se remains *the single most powerful risk factor* for child abuse that has yet been identified."[15] Compared to children in biological homes and even single parent homes, "stepchildren are not merely 'disadvantaged,' but imperiled."[16] What is more, a recent study published in *Pediatrics* (and in the *same* volume in which Perrin's "Technical Report" was published!) indicated that children residing in a home with a stepparent were eight times more likely to *die* of maltreatment than children living with their two biological parents.[17]

These factors indicate why an article in *Psychology Today* concluded: "stepfamilies are such a minefield of divided loyalties, emotional traps, and management conflicts that they are the most fragile form of family in America."[18] Nevertheless, the AAP, through their "Technical Report," actually encourages creating more of these kinds of problems and dangers for children by creating more same-sex parented homes "that closely resemble stepfamilies."

We wonder whether the AAP carefully examined these studies before they published their report, because by implication, same-sex parent families will imperil children.

This research on stepfamilies answers a popular platitude of same-sex family advocates. If "love makes a family" then these stepfamilies, most of whom certainly have deep love, would not show the kinds of pathologies they do. None of the studies outlining these serious problems in stepfamilies attributes them to lack of love among the members. They do attribute the problems however to the adults trying to make a new marital relationship work and a lack of biological connection between the children and one of the parents. These homes have two loving parents—even a loving mother

---

[14]Martin Daly and Margo Wilson, "Child Abuse and Other Risks of Not Living with Both Parents," *Ethology and Sociobiology* 6 (1985): 197-210.

[15]Martin Daly and Margo Wilson, *Homicide* (New York: Aldine de Gruyter, 1988), pp. 87-88 (emphasis added).

[16]Margo Wilson and Martin Daly, "Risk of Maltreatment of Children Living With Stepparents," in *Child Abuse and Neglect: Biosocial Dimensions*, ed. R. Gelles and J. Lancaster (New York: Aldine de Gruyter, 1987), p. 230.

[17]Michael Stiffman et al., "Household Composition and Risk of Fatal Child Maltreatment," *Pediatrics* 109 (2002), 615-21.

[18]"Shuttle Diplomacy," *Psychology Today*, July-August 1993, p. 15.

and father. But they don't provide the child's original mother *and* father. And we understand that same-sex homes will look similar to stepfamily homes because both lack a biological connection between at least one parent and the child. But this is exactly what the AAP is willing to recognize. They just have not recognized or admitted the associated dangers to children.[19]

2. *Research on children of divorce.* But the AAP didn't stop with children of stepfamilies. They said that children "of divorced lesbian mothers grow up in ways very similar to children of divorced heterosexual mothers."[20] It isn't at all clear why divorced heterosexual mothers should serve as the standard of comparison, as the ideal, if we want to know what form of family is best for children.

For the past thirty years, we have seen unprecedented numbers of young people being raised by divorced parents. This has provided researchers with a rich opportunity to study large groups of young people experiencing parental divorce over a long period of time. Dr. Judith Wallerstein (University of California at Berkeley) and Dr. Mavis Hetherington (University of Virginia) are two scholars who have studied the impact of divorce on children since the early 1970s. They are the Bill Gates and Steve Jobs of divorce research, their studies being longer and deeper than any such work in the world. They both conclude that divorce affects children more dramatically and for longer periods of time than scholars and child psychologists ever imagined.

In her thirty-year study, Hetherington found "divorce is usually brutally painful to a child" and that 25 percent of adult children of divorce con-

---

[19]Someone might ask, "Adoption, of course, does not provide children with both biological parents either, but we allow this. Why?" Simply because adoption is a heroic effort of a couple to provide a mother and father and loving home for a child who does not have this. As such, it is an exceptional act, and no one is saying that adoption is just as good for a child as living with both biological parents, assuming that they could provide a good home. Adoption is a wonderful and selfless act of charity, but it can never become a social norm, as same-sex advocates are arguing for same-sex families, which is largely a selfish act. It wouldn't be a good thing for everyone to raise everyone else's child, just as it wouldn't be a good thing for every child to be separated from his or her biological parents and placed in a same-sex home. Biological mothers and fathers raising their own biological children is the ideal. When the ideal is not attainable for some reason, adoption by married mothers and fathers is a loving and heroic alternative. It is the next-best thing. Same-sex parenting is not.

[20]Perrin, "Technical Report," p. 342.

tinue to have "serious social, emotional, and psychological problems" whereas only 10 percent of adult children from intact families had such problems.[21]

When Wallerstein began her twenty-five-year study in the early 1970s, she assumed, along with most scholars, that divorce was a short-lived bump in the road for children. They would recover and move on with their lives. However, she found "divorce is a long-term crisis that was affecting the psychological profile of an entire generation."[22] She reported that almost half the children she observed were "worried, underachieving, self-deprecating, and sometimes angry." Wallerstein explains these children "spoke of divorce as having cut their life short."[23]

Specifically, Wallerstein warns that

children in postdivorce families do not, on the whole, look happier, healthier, or more well adjusted even if one or both parents are happier. National studies show that children from divorced and remarried families are more aggressive toward their parents and teachers. They experience more depression, have more learning difficulties, and suffer from more problems with peers than children from intact families. Children from divorced and remarried families are two to three times more likely to be referred for psychological help at school than their peers from intact families. More of them end up in mental health clinics and hospital settings. There is earlier sexual activity, more children born out of wedlock, less marriage, and more divorce. Numerous studies show that adult children of divorce have more psychological problems than those raised in intact marriages.[24]

If children raised in same-sex households look like children raised in

---

[21]E. Mavis Hetherington, *For Better or For Worse: Divorce Reconsidered* (New York: W. W. Norton, 2002), p. 7.

[22]Judith Wallerstein et al., *The Unexpected Legacy of Divorce: A 25 Year Landmark Study* (New York: Hyperion, 2000), p. xxvii.

[23]Judith Wallerstein, "The Long-Term Effects of Divorce on Children: A Review," *Journal of the American Academy of Child and Adolescent Psychiatry* 30 (1991): 349-60.

[24]Wallerstein, *Unexpected Legacy of Divorce,* p. xxiii.

step- and divorced families, as the AAP "Technical Report" itself asserts, there is little research to indicate that this can be a healthy picture for children. Research indicates the picture is deeply negative and, in some important ways, life-threatening. This is certainly not something we want to create more of, and it certainly offers no cause for comfort with the same-sex family experiment.

QUESTION 5. *So how reliable is the research comparing children who grow up in same-sex or natural mother-father families?*

ANSWER. While the research showing how children fare when they grow up in fatherless, step- or divorced families is very strong, the research that actually compares outcomes in child well-being in straight and homosexual homes is notoriously inconclusive. The reason for this is simple: our nation has had a massive social experiment with unmarried childbearing, divorce, fatherlessness and cohabitation, giving social scientists large populations of children to study over long periods of time. This opportunity allows them to draw strong, informed conclusions. We have not had a long time to study large populations of people in the same-sex-family experiment yet—the experiment is just beginning—so scientists don't have good samples to study. Consider the following surveys of the current literature.

Steven Nock, professor of sociology at the University of Virginia and a member of the editorial board of *Journal of Marriage and the Family,* was asked to review the body of comparative literature for the Ontario Superior Court of Justice. His affidavit states that the current literature on lesbian mothering "is inadequate to permit any conclusions to be drawn. None had a probability sample. All used inappropriate statistics given the samples obtained. All had biased samples. Sample sizes were consistently small. . . . I do not believe this collection of articles indicates that lesbian and heterosexual mothers are similar. In fact, from a scientific perspective, the evidence confirms nothing about the quality of gay parents."[25]

Nock continues, "From a sound methodological perspective, the results

---

[25]Affidavit of Steven L. Nock, *Halpern et al. v. The Attorney General of Canada*, Ontario Superior Court of Justice, March 2001, Court File No. 684/00, pars. 130-131.

of these studies can be relied on for one purpose—to indicate that further research . . . is warranted. . . . The only acceptable conclusion at this point is that the literature on this topic does not constitute a solid body of scientific evidence."[26]

Another recent study in the *Journal of Marriage and the Family*, analyzing the current research on homosexual parenting, finds that "a persistent limitation of these studies, however, is that most rely on small samples of White, middle-class, previously married lesbians and their children. As a result, we cannot be confident concerning the generalizability of many of the findings."[27]

The *American Sociological Review*, in a 2001 study examining the current body of research, explains that it is currently "impossible to fully distinguish the impact of parent's sexual orientation on a child." They explain: because homosexual child-rearing homes can't produce their own natural children, those in these studies didn't start out fresh from birth but are clouded by the dynamics of divorce, remating and stepparenting issues that are problematic in themselves and separate from issues related to gender of the parents. These scholars "disagree with those who claim that there are no differences between the children of heterosexual parents and children of lesbigay parents."[28]

However, these researchers, who are personally sympathetic with the idea of the same-sex family, are honest enough to explain that some studies find that problems with gender identity and sexual exploration could be greater for children raised by homosexual parents than any of the previous studies recognize.[29] Specifically, as we saw earlier, this *American Sociological Review* article highlights research indicating that 64 percent of young adults raised by lesbian mothers reported considering having same-sex erotic relationships either in the past, now or in the future. Only 17 percent of young adults in heterosexual families reported the same thing. These authors explain there is "evidence of a moderate degree of parent-

---

[26]Ibid., pars. 140-41.

[27]David Demo and Martha Cox, "Families with Young Children: A Review of Research in the 1990s," *Journal of Marriage and the Family* 62 (2000): 889.

[28]Judith Stacey and Timothy Biblarz, "(How) Does the Sexual Orientation of Parents Matter?" *American Sociological Review* 66 (2001): 159-83.

[29]Ibid., p. 167.

to-child transmission of sexual orientation."[30]

So, should we subject large populations of children to this new experiment so we can learn whether it will harm them or not? Wouldn't that be treating children like lab rats? No compassionate society treats children this way. We can be quite certain what will happen. When you deny children either their mother or their father, even if one is replaced with another loving but nonbiologically connected parent, the children suffer in deep and unexpected ways. Data over the past few decades show this to be undeniably true because millions of children have been subjected to such families for decades.

CONCLUSION

Contrary to the AAP's claim, there actually is no basis for saying that children in mom-and-dad homes look just like kids from same-sex homes in terms of important well-being outcomes. This is because the Academy's "Technical Report" subtly communicates caution in endorsing same-sex parenting due to the methodological problems in the research. Their conclusion is that children from same-sex parenting homes "closely resemble stepfamilies" and "are very similar to children of divorce,"[31] which research indicates is not good. Research is clear that the best course of action for accomplishing optimal health for all children is to reduce, rather than encourage, the number of children being raised apart from their mothers and fathers. It is therefore not smart to encourage same-sex parenting.

---

[30]Ibid., pp. 170-71.
[31]Perrin, "Technical Report," pp. 341-42.

CHEAT SHEET FOR SECTION I

By legalizing same-sex marriage, we lose . . .

1. the unique value of male and female

- Male same-sex marriage says women are not necessary for the family.
- Female same-sex marriage says men are not necessary for the family.
- A same-sex family says kids don't need mothers or fathers.

On a social and cultural level, every same-sex family fails to understand that:

- Men need women to domesticate them and channel their masculine and sexual energy in socially productive ways.
- A woman needs a man to protect her from exploitation of other unattached men.
- A man who is permanently committed to one woman is not a man who is likely to sexually pressure or even threaten other women.

These are universal, sociological human rules.

2. the special value of your marriage

The same-sex marriage proposal permanently alters the definition of marriage for everyone, forever. It robs everyone of us of the special value and wonder of our marriages: a marriage where you are serving an essential social and personal good of loving, caring for and completing another human being of the other gender. A natural marriage includes the wonder of a relationship where you are creating and bearing new life together and raising that new life to full and healthy human maturity with his or her other biological parent. Same-sex marriage changes all of this and says none of it matters. It is just mere personal preference.

3. the necessary social value of monogamy

Monogamy, research and experience tells us, is virtually impossible in male homosexual relationships.

If homosexual men can't be expected to be faithful to their "marriages," it will be more difficult to expect heterosexual men to be faithful to their marriages. It is a sociological rule that human behavior tends to run downhill to the lowest—socially tolerated—common denominator.

If same-sex advocates can successfully persuade courts to allow their re-definition of marriage, why couldn't sincere polygamists convince the courts to allow their redefinition of marriage?

Therefore, same-sex marriage will very likely encourage society to see monogamy as optional.

4. the dignity and status of women

If two married men are morally equal to a married man and a woman, then the social value of a husband—the good family man who cares for and pro-tects his wife and children—is lost as a social ideal. More women will be left to fend for themselves.

Same-sex marriage could lead to polygamy, and anthropologists consis-tently tell us that women, especially younger women, in polygamous cultures become commodities, exploited and collected as possessions by older men.

Research by Scott Coltrane shows us that societies with lower rates of fa-ther involvement in the lives of their children have lower respect and pro-vide less significant social opportunity for women. Lesbian families could unwittingly be harming the standing of women in society by creating more fatherless families.

Monogamous marriage is the great domestic and social equalizer.

5. the well-being and safety of children

Every same-sex union with a child intentionally denies that child a mother or a father, and that is never compassionate.

Children are put at serious risk of physical and sexual abuse when they live in a family with a nonbiological parent. Therefore, all same-sex parent-ing potentially puts children at serious risk.

Same sex marriage teaches children that husband and wife, father and mother, male and female are mere words, robbing them of a true under-standing of the complexity and wonder of their humanity.

6. the right to religious conviction and democracy

When it is established that gay marriage is a "fundamental human right," it is reasonable that it will be taught as normal in every public school. Pictures and story lines in textbooks will be changed to reflect this dramatic social change. Churches could be pressured to perform same-sex weddings or risk losing their tax-exempt status. Doesn't it seem likely that groups like the ACLU will successfully argue that the government is underwriting discrimination by extending tax-exempt status to churches that won't recognize same-sex couple's "fundamental right" to marry?

Your right to oppose homosexuality, or to oppose it being taught to other children in school, and to preach and teach against it in church could be lost. It could become hate speech to say children need a mother and a father. Months after passing same-sex marriage in Canada, its national parliament passed C-250, a bill criminalizing "hate-speech" against homosexuals, punishable by up to two years in prison. Similar things could happen in other countries.

7. the mechanism that delivers the next healthy, productive, safe generation
When there is no special value to (1) males and females permanently committing to, sacrificing for and completing each other, and (2) biological, procreative childbearing and rearing, then we erase the mechanism that has allowed all civilizations to bring forth the next healthy, socially productive, compassionate and considerate generation. We lose this if all relationships are seen as equal, for no society has been able to sustain itself with a smorgasbord mentality to family life—pick what appeals to you and all choices are equally good.

REMINDER FOR THE DEBATE

Marriage is a gift to us from God. It is his institution that he has given to all of humanity. As you prepare to engage friends, neighbors and even opponents with the purpose of defending marriage, remember that God cares more deeply than any of us for the institution of marriage. (He also cares deeply for those who feel they must redefine it.) This is not your fight; it is God's. Allow him to use you in defending it. Defend natural marriage with confidence and compassion. And keep your eye on the prize of graciously and lovingly winning to Christ those who seek to change marriage. We honor God by defending the glory of marriage and loving those who are struggling under the burden of sexual confusion.

UNDERSTANDING HOW MARRIAGE MATTERS TO ADULTS, CHILDREN AND SOCIETY

In the first section we addressed the main reasons why same-sex marriage and parenting are not good ideas. But in making a case against this ill-advised proposal, we have only done half the job.

We must now show how natural marriage uniquely provides real, tangible benefits for adults, children and society as a whole, and thus why every society finds it necessary. This will establish why it is necessary to keep marriage as a permanent union of one man and one woman. We then have to ask what it is about marriage that provides these rich benefits. We will find that the benefit-producing value of marriage is found in the way it brings men and women together.

8

How Does Marriage Benefit Adults?

What if you found that you unknowingly possessed something of incredibly deep value—something that you held precious in a sentimental way but then discovered had a measurable worth in a far grander way than you ever imagined? No doubt you would care for and protect it from harm and devaluation. Marriage is just such a treasure. Many think it is merely a sentimental relationship between two people, but it's really much more than this—a deep personal and social good. In this chapter, through the findings of more than one hundred years of social-science research, we will explore the unexpected social and personal riches of marriage for adults.

QUESTION 1. *Is marriage simply an emotional relationship between two people, or does it have real, measurable social value?*

ANSWER. Over the past few decades huge amounts of research have been published on how family breakdown affects people. In this research, scholars are finding that marriage has a much greater affect on our lives than many have assumed. This is especially true in the area of adult health and well-being. Sociologist Linda Waite and researcher Maggie Gallagher explain, "The evidence from four decades of research is surprisingly clear: a good marriage is both men's and women's best bet for living a long and healthy life."[1]

This powerful body of scientific inquiry reveals that men and women who are in their first marriages, on average, enjoy significantly higher levels of physical and mental health than their peers in *any* other relational cate-

---

[1]Linda J. Waite and Maggie Gallagher, *The Case for Marriage: Why Married People Are Happier, Healthier, and Better-Off Financially* (New York: Doubleday, 2000), p. 64.

gory. Leading social scientist James Q. Wilson explains:

> Married people are happier than unmarried ones of the same age, not
> only in the United States, but in at least seventeen other countries
> where similar inquiries have been made. And there seems to be good
> reasons for that happiness. People who are married not only have
> higher incomes and enjoy greater emotional support, they tend to be
> healthier. Married people live longer than unmarried ones, not only in
> the United States but abroad.[2]

Research conducted at the University of Massachusetts concludes, "One
of the most consistent observations in health research is that the married enjoy better health than those of other [relational] statuses."[3]

Dr. Robert Coombs of UCLA reviewed more than 130 empirical studies
published in this century on how marriage affects well-being. He found
these studies indicate "an intimate link between marital status and personal
well-being."[4] Being married has a very positive impact on some important
well-being categories that we explore in this chapter.

Professor George Akerlof, in a prestigious lecture a few years ago, high-
lighted compelling research that indicates the socializing influence of marriage for men. He explained, "Married men are more attached to the labor
force, they have less substance abuse, they commit less crime, are less likely
to become the victims of crime, have better health, and are less accident
prone." He found cohabitation was incapable of providing these benefits.
Akerlof explains this is because "men settle down when they get married and
if they fail to get married, they fail to settle down."[5] Married men make better neighbors and citizens. And as historian Gail Collins explains in her book
America's Women, one of the most important social roles women play in his-

---

[2]James Q. Wilson, *The Marriage Problem: How Our Culture Has Weakened Families* (New York: Harper Collins, 2002), p. 16.
[3]Katherine Reissman and Naomi Gerstel, "Marital Dissolution and Health: Do Males or Females Have Greater Risk?" *Social Science and Medicine* 20 (1985): 627-35.
[4]Robert Coombs, "Marital Status and Personal Well-Being: A Literature Review," *Family Relations* 40 (1991): 97-102.
[5]George A. Akerlof, "Men Without Children," *The Economic Journal* 108 (1998): 287-309.

tory is "getting men to behave" by channeling their passions and work behaviors in socially productive ways.[6] In fact, anthropologist Margaret Mead argues that a major challenge any culture has is to civilize its male population through marriage.[7]

Monogamous marriage socializes men by giving women socially enforced—and exclusive—claims on men. Same-sex marriage says that it is not important for men to permanently link themselves to women. It says anyone—male or female—will do. It says marriage is simply about emotional feelings any two people have for one another. But marriage is much more than this because it is the one social institution that successfully bridges the divide of humanity and brings the genders together in a respectful, loving and cooperative relationship.

QUESTION 2. *In what specific areas of life do male-female marriages benefit adults?*

ANSWER. Let's start with how it leads to a longer, healthier life.

Unmarried people have lower activity levels, and they spend *twice* as much time as patients in hospitals as their married peers.[8] Research conducted at Erasmus University in Rotterdam reports that "married people have the lowest morbidity [illness] rates, while the divorced show the highest."[9] Professor Linda Waite of the University of Chicago finds that the "relationship between marriage and death rates has now reached the status of a truism, having been observed across numerous societies and among various social and demographic groups."[10]

In Waite's 1995 presidential address to the Population Association of

---

[6]Gail Gollins, *America's Women: 400 Years of Dolls, Drudges, Helpmates and Heroines* (New York: William Morrow, 2003), pp. 3-14, 316-24.

[7]Margaret Mead, *Male and Female: A Study of the Sexes in a Changing World* (New York: William Morrow, 1949), pp. 5-6, 183-200.

[8]Lois Verbrugge and Donald Balaban, "Patterns of Change, Disability and Well-Being," *Medical Care* 27 (1989): S128-S147.

[9]I. M. Joung et al., "Differences in Self-Reported Morbidity by Marital Status and by Living Arrangement," *International Journal of Epidemiology* 23 (1994): 91-97.

[10]Linda J. Waite, "Does Marriage Matter?" the presidential address to the American Population Association of America, San Francisco, April 8, 1995; Linda Waite, "Does Marriage Matter?" *Demography* 32 (1995): 483-507.

America, she explained that the health benefits of marriage are so strong that a married man with heart disease can be expected to live, on average, 1,400 days longer (nearly four years) than an unmarried man with a healthy heart. This longer life expectancy is even greater for a married man who has cancer or is twenty pounds overweight compared to his healthy but unmarried counterpart. Being unmarried will shave more days off a woman's life than being married and having cancer, being twenty pounds overweight or having a low socioeconomic status. Additional research from Yale University indicates that a married man who smokes more than a pack a day can be expected to live as long as a divorced man who does not smoke. This researcher explains with a touch of humor, "If a man's marriage is driving him to heavy smoking, he has a delicate statistical decision to make."[11]

Robert Coombs's research agrees with these findings: "Virtually every study of mortality and marital status shows the unmarried of both sexes have higher death rates, whether by accident, disease, or self-inflicted wounds, and this is found in every country that maintains accurate health statistics."[12]

Research published in the *Journal of the American Medical Association* finds that cures for cancer are significantly more successful (8 to 17 percent) when a patient is married, and being married was comparable to being in an age category ten years younger.[13]

Marriage is more than just an emotional relationship. It is a very real fountain of youth.

QUESTION 3. *But isn't marriage often a source of mental stress, especially for women?*

ANSWER. Quite the opposite. Just as marriage increases physical health, it also benefits mental health.

Men and women who wear wedding bands report significantly decreased levels of depression, less anxiety and less of any other type of psy-

---

[11]Harold Morowitz, "Hiding in the Hammond Report," *Hospital Practice,* August 1975, p. 39.
[12]Coombs, "Marital Status and Personal Well-Being," p. 98.
[13]James Goodwin et al., "The Effect of Marital Status on Stage, Treatment, and Survival of Cancer Patients," *Journal of the American Medical Association* 258 (1987): 3130-52.

chological distress than those who are single, divorced or widowed.[14] Research dating back to 1936 shows that first-time psychiatric admission rates for males suffering from schizophrenia were 5.4 times greater for unmarried men than for married men. Dr. Benjamin Malzberg, the author of this study, concludes, "The evidence seems clear that the married population had, in general, much lower rates of mental disease than any of the other marital groups."[15]

More recent research conducted jointly at Yale University and UCLA reports:

> One of the most consistent findings in psychiatric epidemiology is that married persons enjoy better health than the unmarried. Researchers have consistently found the highest rates of mental disorder among the divorced and separated, the lowest rates among the married and intermediate rates among the single and widowed. They also found that a cohabiting partner could not replicate these benefits of marriage.[16]

QUESTION 4. *Are you saying that married people, with all the responsibilities of a relationship and family, are happier than people who are free to move from relationship to relationship?*

ANSWER. Research says exactly that! A study published in the *Journal of Marriage and the Family* examined the link between personal happiness and marital status in seventeen industrialized nations that had "diverse social and institutional frameworks," or in plain language "all kinds of different cultures." This study found that

> married persons have a significantly higher level of happiness than persons who are not married. This effect was independent of financial and health-oriented protections offered by marriage and was also in-

---

[14]John Mirowsky and Catherine E. Ross, *Social Causes of Psychological Distress* (New York: Aldine de Gruyter, 1989), pp. 90-92.

[15]Benjamin Malzberg, "Marital Status in Relation to the Prevalence of Mental Disease," *Psychiatric Quarterly* 10 (1936): 245-61.

[16]David Williams et al., "Marital Status and Psychiatric Disorders Among Blacks and Whites," *Journal of Health and Social Behavior* 33 (1992): 140-57.

dependent of other control variables including ones for sociodemo-
graphic conditions and national character.[17]

Increased levels of happiness among the married were found in other
studies as well.[18] A survey of 14,000 adults measured over a ten-year period
found that marital status was one of the strongest indicators of happiness,
with the married being the happiest, generally, and the divorced being the
most unhappy, even behind the widowed.[19]

QUESTION 5. *Are there other benefits to marriage for adults?*

ANSWER. Yes, quite a few. Consider the following:

1. *Substance abuse.* Seventy percent of chronic problem drinkers are either divorced or separated, and only 15 percent are married. Single men
are more than three times as likely to die of cirrhosis of the liver compared
with married men.[20] Married people (and even those who are engaged)
smoke, drink and use cocaine and marijuana at much lower rates than
their unmarried peers.[21]

2. *Sexual fulfillment.* Married people—both men and women—report the
absolute highest levels of physically and emotionally fulfilling sex lives.[22]

3. *Loneliness.* Married people are significantly less likely to report feeling
lonely.[23]

4. *Domestic violence.* Marriage dramatically protects women from sexual,

---

[17]Steven Stack and J. Ross Eshleman, "Marital Status and Happiness: A 17-Nation Study," *Journal of Marriage and the Family* 60 (1998): 527-36.

[18]Coombs, "Marital Status and Personal Well-Being," p. 100.

[19]James A. Davis, "New Money, an Old Man/Lady, and 'Twos Company': Subjective Welfare in
the NORC General Social Survey, 1972-1982," *Social Indicators Research* 15 (1984): 319-50.
Also derived from tabulations by Linda J. Waite from the General Social Survey, 1990-1996
waves.

[20]Coombs, "Marital Status and Personal Well-Being," p. 97.

[21]Waite and Gallagher, *Case for Marriage,* pp. 54-55.

[22]Robert T. Michael et al., *Sex in America: A Definitive Survey* (Boston: Little, Brown, 1994), pp.
124-29; Edward O. Laumann et al., *The Social Organization of Sexuality: Sexual Practices in the
United States* (Chicago: University of Chicago Press, 1994), p. 364, table 10.5; Andrew Greeley, *Faithful Attraction: Discovering Intimacy, Love and Fidelity in American Marriage* (New York:
Tom Doherty, 1991), chap. 6.

[23]Randy Page and Galen Cole, "Demographic Predictors of Self-Reported Loneliness in Adults,"
Psychological Reports 68 (1991): 939-45.

domestic and general violence.[24] Only about 1.7 percent of wives and about 0.75 percent of husbands are attacked and injured by their spouse in a year.[25]

5. *Better parents.* Marriage enhances a parent's ability and enjoyment of parenting.[26]

6. *Better on the job.* Marriage helps create better, more reliable employees who miss fewer days of work, are more productive while there and are less likely to skip from job to job.[27] The research on this point led George Akerlof to conclude, "the job performance of married employees appears to be significantly better than the job performance of single employees."[28]

7. *Show me the money.* Marriage increases people's individual earnings and savings.[29]

QUESTION 6. *Why do scholars believe marriage provides these benefits?*

ANSWER. Research conducted at the University of Colorado indicates why marriage is so beneficial to adults. Generally, compared with those who are not married, married individuals eat better, take better care of themselves and live a more stable, secure and scheduled lifestyle.[30] Clearly, married men and women provide better things for society than their unmarried peers in profound and measurable ways.

Because of their better health and increased ability to recover from illness more successfully, husbands and wives are not as likely to be a burden to the healthcare system or be a drain on a company's health insurance benefits.

---

[24]Jan Stets, "Cohabiting and Marital Aggression: The Role of Social Isolation," *Journal of Marriage and the Family* 53 (1991): 669-80; "Criminal Victimization in the United States, 1992," U.S. Department of Justice, Office of Justice Programs, Bureau of Justice Statistics NCJ-145125 (March 1994), p. 31.

[25]Linda Waite's tabulations from the National Survey of Families and Households, 1987-1988, as cited in Waite and Gallagher, *Case for Marriage,* p. 153.

[26]Ronald Angel and Jacqueline Angel, *Painful Inheritance: Health and the New Generation of Fatherless Families* (Madison: University of Wisconsin Press, 1993), pp. 139, 148.

[27]Janet Wilmoth and Gregor Koso, "Does Marital History Matter? Marital Status and Wealth Outcomes Among Pre-retirement Adults," *Journal of Marriage and the Family* 64 (2002): 743-54.

[28]Akerlof, "Men Without Children," p. 304.

[29]Waite, "Does Marriage Matter?" pp. 483-507. Waite and Gallagher, *Case for Marriage,* chap. 8; Wilmoth and Koso, "Does Marital History Matter?" pp. 743-54.

[30]Richard Rogers, "Marriage, Sex, and Mortality," *Journal of Marriage and the Family* 57 (1995): 515-26.

They are less likely to miss work because of illness. They are not likely to jump from job to job. They are less likely to be alcoholics or abuse other substances and less likely to engage in other risk behaviors. Married women are significantly less likely to be victims of any kind of violence, either by her spouse or by a stranger. They are less lonely and are happier. Happier people make better citizens, employees and neighbors. Married people earn and invest more money. They report enjoying parenting, and they are more successful at it. This mountain of social-science research tells us marriage is a serious and valuable community treasure for adults.

Why does marriage accomplish these good things for people and society? These studies reveal that marriage is the one institution that brings men and women together in their differences and qualities, and helps them build a lifelong bond in which each seeks to serve and complete the other. Every society needs this to happen. There is no reason to believe or evidence to suggest that bringing two men or two women together in "marriage" will provide any of these necessary social goods.

CONCLUSION

Heterosexual men and women who are married do better in every important measure of well-being than their peers in any other marital category. Marriage makes people better citizens and employees, and they provide more benefits for the community and workplace than they take from it. Every growing, healthy, productive society needs this to happen, and nothing does it like natural marriage.

9

How Does Marriage Benefit Children?

A most basic measure of the goodness of any society is how it cares for its children. When society debates what children need to grow into healthy, happy, productive and well-adjusted adults, many things are listed as essentials: access to healthcare, nutrition, good schools, safe neighborhoods, love and plenty of encouragement. All of these are important to healthy child development, but the discussion often ignores the one factor that's more vital than all these others: a married mother and father. If we are going to be concerned with the health and well-being of our children, as we will see in this chapter, we must be concerned about the health and well-being of marriage.

QUESTION 1. *Marriage provides benefits to the man and woman who are married, but does it provide real benefits to children?*

ANSWER. All things being equal, children with married parents consistently do better in every measure of well-being than their peers in any other type of family arrangement. And this is a stronger indicator of well-being than the race, economic or educational status of parents, or of the neighborhood in which these children grow up. The research supporting these conclusions is very robust.

Pitirim Sorokin, founder and first chair of the sociology department at Harvard University, proclaimed the importance of married mothers and fathers some sixty years ago:

> The most essential sociocultural patterning of a newborn human organism is achieved by the family. It is the first and most efficient sculptor of human material, shaping the physical, behavioral, mental, moral and sociocultural characteristics of practically every individual.

. . . From remotest past, married parents have been the most effective teachers of their children.[1]

Research over the past few decades only confirms this idea. The child advocacy organization *Center for Law and Social Policy* (CLASP) recently reported: "Most researchers now agree that . . . studies support the notion that, on average, children do best when raised by their two married biological parents."[2] *Child Trends* also reports: "An extensive body of research tells us that children do best when they grow up with both biological parents."[3]

QUESTION 2. *Specifically, how do children benefit when they grow up with their biological mothers and fathers?*

ANSWER. Sara McLanahan of Princeton University, one of the world's leading scholars on how family formation affects child well-being, finds that regardless of which survey we look at, children raised with only one biological parent are about twice as likely to drop out of school as children being raised with two biological parents.[4] Children from married two-parent families, on average, have test scores and grade-point averages that are higher, they miss fewer school days, and they have greater expectations of attending college than children living with one parent. Additionally, of those from either type of family who do attend college, those from biological two-parent families are 7 to 20 percent more likely to finish college.[5]

Children from divorced homes are 70 percent more likely than those living with biological parents to be expelled or suspended from school. Those living with never-married mothers are twice as likely to be expelled or suspended. In addition, children who don't live with both biological parents are significantly more likely to require parent-teacher meetings to deal with per-

[1]Pitirim Sorokin, *Society, Culture, and Personality* (New York: Harper & Row, 1947), pp. 246-47; and his *The American Sex Revolution* (Boston: Porter Sargent, 1956), p. 5.

[2]Mary Parke, "Are Married Parents Really Better for Children?" *Center for Law and Social Policy Policy Brief,* May 2003, p. 1.

[3]Kristin Anderson Moore et al., "Marriage From a Child's Perspective: How Does Family Structure Affect Children, and What Can We Do About It?" *Child Trends Research Brief,* June 2002, p. 1.

[4]Sara McLanahan and Gary Sandefur, *Growing Up with a Single Parent: What Hurts, What Helps* (Cambridge, Mass.: Harvard University Press, 1994), p. 19.

[5]Ibid., p. 47.

formance or behavior problems than those who live with married parents.[6]

Likewise, young men without married parents are 1.5 times more likely than those with married parents to be out of school and out of work. Young girls without married parents are twice as likely to be out of school and not working.[7]

QUESTION 3. *How else do married parents help children?*

ANSWER. Marriage reduces crime. Research from Stanford University on factors contributing to crime in a community explains: "Such family measures as the percentages of the population divorced, the percentages of households headed by women, and the percentage of unattached individuals in the community are among the most powerful predictors of crime rates."[8] The Progressive Policy Institute, the research arm of the Democratic Leadership Council, reported that the relationship between crime and fatherless families is "so strong that controlling for family configuration erases the relationship between race and crime and between low-income and crime. This conclusion shows up time and again in the literature."[9]

Married moms and dads also help kids avoid premarital sex and childbearing. A major study published in the *Journal of Marriage and the Family* found that boys and girls who lived with both biological parents had the lowest risk of becoming sexually active. Teens living with only one biological parent, *including those in stepfamilies,* were particularly at risk for becoming sexually active at younger ages.[10] Compare this to one of the studies we examined in chapter seven that indicates that "girls raised by lesbian mothers appear to have been more sexually adventurous and less chaste." And they

[6]Deborah Dawson, "Family Structure and Children's Health and Well-Being: Data from the 1988 National Health Interview Survey on Child Health," *Journal of Marriage and the Family* 53 (1991): 573-84.

[7]McLanahan and Sandefur, *Growing Up with a Single Parent*, p. 50.

[8]Michael Gottfredson and Travis Hirschi, *A General Theory of Crime* (Stanford, Calif.: Stanford University Press, 1990), p. 103.

[9]Elaine Kamarck and William Galston, "Putting Children First: A Progressive Family Policy for the 1990s," white paper from the Progressive Policy Institute, September 27, 1990, pp. 14-15.

[10]Dawn Upchurch et al., "Neighborhood and Family Contexts of Adolescent Sexual Activity," *Journal of Marriage and the Family* 61 (1999): 920-30.

are more likely to be involved sexually with other girls.[11]

Sara McLanahan found that white and black girls growing up without fathers in their homes are 111 percent more likely to bear children as teenagers, 164 percent more likely to have a child out of marriage and—if they do marry—their marriages are 92 percent more likely to dissolve when compared to their counterparts with married parents.[12]

QUESTION 4. *Poverty is such a harmful thing for children. Does marriage affect this?*

ANSWER. Historically, poverty for children has been a result of unemployment and low wages earned by parents. Today, it is primarily a result of not having married parents. David Ellwood, professor of public policy at Harvard University, notes: "The vast majority of children who are raised entirely in a home where parents are married will never be poor during childhood. By contrast, the vast majority of children who spend time in a fatherless home will experience poverty."[13] The Progressive Policy Institute declares: "It is no exaggeration to say that a stable, two-parent family is an American child's best protection against poverty."[14]

In fact, former domestic policy adviser in the Clinton administration, Dr. Bill Galston, explains that avoiding family poverty requires three things: (1) finishing high school, (2) marrying before having children and (3) marrying after the age of twenty. Only 8 percent of families who do these are poor, while 79 percent of those who fail to do these are poor.[15] Children with married mothers and fathers are more likely to do all of these things and therefore are not likely to raise children who also end up in poverty. Marriage breaks the vicious poverty cycle that traps generation after generation of children.

---

[11]Judith Stacey and Timothy Biblarz, "(How) Does the Sexual Orientation of Parents Matter?" *American Sociological Review* 66 (2001): 170-71.

[12]Irwin Garfinkel and Sara McLanahan, *Single Mothers and Their Children: A New American Dilemma* (Washington, D.C.: Urban Institute Press, 1986), pp. 30-31.

[13]David Ellwood, *Poor Support: Poverty in the American Family* (New York: Basic Books, 1988), p. 46.

[14]Kamarck and Galston, "Putting Children First," p. 12.

[15]James Q. Wilson, "Why We Don't Marry," *City Journal,* Winter 2002, <www.cityjournal.org/html/12_1_why_we.html>.

QUESTION 5. *Marriage improves adult health. Does it improve child health?*

ANSWER. Yes, in very strong ways. Mothers raising kids without fathers report poorer overall physical health for their children than do mothers in intact marriages, regardless of racial or ethnic status.[16]

The National Center for Health Statistics found that children living with their biological parents received professional help for behavior and psychological problems at *half* the rate of children not living with both biological parents.[17] Other studies show the general health problems of children from fatherless families is increased by 20 to 30 percent, even when adjusting for demographic variables such as race, income and neighborhood.[18]

Dr. Judith Wallerstein, a leading authority on the long-term effects of divorce on children, found that serious emotional and relational problems follow children of divorce throughout adolescence into adulthood. In fact, in some important measures the negative effects of parental divorce grow worse as the child enters adulthood.[19] Dr. Nicholas Zill, writing in the *Journal of Family Psychology*, agrees, finding that children of divorce showed "high levels of emotional distress, or problem behavior, [and were more likely] to have received psychological help."[20] Many same-sex homes are created as a result of a homosexual parent leaving an existing marriage via divorce. Destroying a marriage to start another one may be desirable for a parent, but it hurts children deeply.

---

[16]Ronald J. Angel and Jacqueline Worobey, "Single Motherhood and Children's Health," *Journal of Health and Social Behavior* 29 (1988): 38-52; Ronald J. Angel and Jacqueline L. Angel, *Painful Inheritance: Health and the New Generation of Fatherless Families* (Madison: University of Wisconsin Press, 1993).

[17]Deborah A. Dawson, "Family Structure and Children's Health and Well-Being: Data from the National Health Interview Survey on Child Health," *Journal of Marriage and the Family* 53 (1991): 573-84.

[18]L. Remez, "Children Who Don't Live with Both Parents Face Behavioral Problems," *Family Planning Perspectives*, January-February 1992.

[19]Judith Wallerstein and Sandra Blakeslee, *Second Chances: Men and Woman a Decade After Divorce* (New York: Ticknor & Fields, 1990); Judith Wallerstein et al., The *Unexpected Legacy of Divorce: A 25 Year Landmark Study*, (New York: Hyperion, 2000), pp. xxvii-xxix.

[20]Nicholas Zill, Donna Morrison and Mary Jo Coiro, "Long-Term Effects of Parental Divorce on Parent-Child Relationships, Adjustment, and Achievement in Young Adulthood," *Journal of Family Psychology* 7 (1993): 91-103.

QUESTION 6. *How about substance abuse?*

ANSWER. Marriage protects against this for children. Regardless of gender, age, family income, race or ethnicity, adolescents not living with a biological mother or father are 50 to 150 percent more likely to abuse and be dependent on substances, and need illicit-drug-abuse treatment compared to their peers living with both biological parents.[21]

The same study reported that females in mother-only families are 1.9 times more likely to use alcohol as are girls living with both mother and father. Males in mother-only families are 1.5 times more likely to use alcohol than teen males living in mother-father families.

QUESTION 7. *Are there other dangers facing children not living with their biological mothers and fathers?*

ANSWER. Yes. Perhaps one of the most serious is the dramatically increased risk for both physical and sexual abuse. The journal *Pediatrics* reported in 2002 that "Children residing in households with non-biological adults were 8 times more likely to die of maltreatment than children in households with 2 biological parents. Risk of maltreatment death was elevated for children residing with step, foster, or adoptive parents."[22] We must recognize that all children living in same-sex homes are living with a nonbiological parent and this *will*, according to research, increase the potential for serious abuse, neglect and death.

Research published in the journal *Child Abuse and Neglect* found that a girl is seven times more likely to be molested by a stepfather than a biological father. The study goes on to report that when biological fathers did molest their young daughters, a mother, who could protect the child, was not residing in the home. What is more, the nature of sexual abuse by stepfathers, which was more prevalent, was also more severe than by biological fathers.[23]

---

[21]Substance Abuse and Mental Health Services Administration, *The Relationship Between Family Structure and Adolescent Substance Use* (Rockville, Md.: National Clearinghouse for Alcohol and Drug Information, 1996).

[22]Michael Stiffman et al., "Household Composition and Risk of Fatal Child Maltreatment," *Pediatrics* 109 (2002): 615-21.

[23]Michael Gordon, "The Family Environment of Sexual Abuse: A Comparison of Natal and Stepfather Abuse," *Child Abuse and Neglect* 13 (1985): 121-30.

Another study published in the same journal reports that children living with a single biological parent are nearly twice as likely to be sexually abused by someone the family knows compared with a child living with a married mother and father.[24] And a recent ten-year review of child sexual abuse (CSA) shows that "before the late 1970s, CSA was regarded as rare. In the following decades, the incidence—based on official statistics—increased dramatically." What caused this dramatic 67 percent increase during the 1980s and 1990s? These researchers point to a number of reasons, but one of the major factors was "the nature of the relationship between the child and perpetrator."[25] More kids were living in homes with nonbiological parents or adults, therefore more kids were at risk for sexual abuse.

Now after presenting research like this in public debates, our opponents usually respond by saying, "Exactly, and we want to provide children with all these benefits of marriage, but you won't let us! And besides, you are comparing kids in single-parent homes with kids in married homes, which isn't fair." And we have to explain that they have not been paying attention.

It is not just marriage between any two adults that benefits children, but the marriage of their own mothers and fathers. As we have seen in this chapter and elsewhere in this book, stepfamilies—where a biological parent who has left the family is replaced by a nonbiological parent—are not as likely to provide the same rich benefits for children that married biological parents do. Consider again the words of sociologist David Popenoe:

> Stepfamilies typically have an economic advantage, but some recent studies indicate that the children of stepfamilies have as many behavioral and emotional problems as the children of single-parent families, and possibly more. . . .

---

[24]David Finkelhor et al., "Sexually Abused Children in a National Survey of Parents: Methodological Issues," *Child Abuse and Neglect* 21 (1997): 1-9.
[25]Frank Putnam, "Ten Year Research Update Review: Child Sexual Abuse," *Journal of the American Academy of Child and Adolescent Psychiatry* 42 (2003): 269-79.

> Stepfamily problems, in short, may be so intractable that *the best strategy for dealing with them is to do everything possible to minimize their occurrence.*[26]

And these more problematic family forms more closely represent the living situations of children in same-sex homes. This is because most children living in same-sex homes were conceived in a heterosexual relationship that ended and then another, secondary relationship was formed with a nonbiological partner of the same-sex.[27] We should take Dr. Popenoe's sage advice and "do everything possible to minimize [the] occurrence" of such families because they put children at increased risk for serious problems. This data gives us great reason to show caution about entering the same-sex family experiment.

CONCLUSION

Marriage is a rich personal resource for children and their parents. It protects them from poverty and sexual and physical abuse. It improves their physical and mental health. It helps them do better in every measure of educational development, including the encouragement to attend college. It helps them stay away from violent, criminal and sexual behaviors. Marriage protects kids from substance abuse. This means teachers aren't burdened with children who cause problems or have difficulty learning. Marriage protects our welfare systems by reducing the number of young adults who have dropped out of school and aren't working or are having children in their teen years. Kids with married parents rarely are a problem for the police. Marriage produces healthy children who don't place stress on our nation's medical system and insurance costs. *And it's not just marriage that benefits children but the marriage of their biological mothers and fathers, for stepfamilies fail to provide these high levels of benefits.*

---

[26]David Popenoe, "The Evolution of Marriage and the Problems of Stepfamilies: A Biosocial Perspective," in *Stepfamilies: Who Benefits? Who Does Not?* ed. Alan Booth and Judy Dunn (Hillsdale, N.J.: Lawrence Erlbaum, 1994), pp. 5, 19 (emphasis added).

[27]Ellen C. Perrin, "Technical Report: Coparent and Second-Parent Adoption by Same-Sex Parents," *Pediatrics* 109, no. 2 (2002): 341.

If we are going to concern ourselves with the welfare of children, we have to be concerned with the health of marriage in our culture. For as natural marriage goes, so go our children—and with them—the future of humanity.

10

WHY DO CHILDREN
NEED MOTHERS *AND* FATHERS?

Everyone raising a child with someone of the opposite sex knows from daily experience that mothers and fathers parent differently. In fact, mothers and fathers will often argue over their differences in parenting; both believe their way is best, and each tries to convince the other of the fact. In reality both ways matter. No doubt you will recognize many of them in your own family experience, but in this chapter you will gain an understanding of *how* these particular differences benefit your children.

If Heather is being raised by two mommies, and Brandon is being raised by Daddy and his new husband/roommate, they might have two loving adults in their lives, but they are being deprived of the benefits found in the unique influences mothers and fathers provide for children.

Much of the value mothers and fathers bring to their children is due to the fact that mothers and fathers are different. And by cooperating together and complementing each other in their differences, a mother and father team provides these good things that same-sex caregivers can't.

The fathering difference is explained by Dr. Kyle Pruett of Yale Medical School in his book *Fatherneed: Why Father Care Is as Essential as Mother Care for Your Child.* Pruett explains dads matter simply because "fathers do not mother."[1] *Psychology Today* notes, "fatherhood turns out to be a complex and unique phenomenon with huge consequences for the emotional and intel-

---

[1]See Kyle D. Pruett, *Fatherneed: Why Father Care Is as Essential as Mother Care for Your Child* (New York: Free Press, 2000), pp. 17-34.

lectual growth of children."[2] A scientific review of over one hundred published studies on the benefits of child-parent relationships summarizes: "Overall, father love appears to be as heavily implicated as mother love in offsprings' psychological well-being and health."[3] A father, as a male parent, brings unique contributions to the job of parenting that a mother can't.

In *The Power of Mother Love,* Dr. Brenda Hunter likewise observes that a mother, as a female parent, uniquely affects the life and development of her child.[4] Father love and mother love are qualitatively different kinds of love according to Erik Erikson. Fathers "love more dangerously" because their love is more "expectant, more instrumental" than a mother's love.[5]

QUESTION 1. *Okay, mothers and fathers are different in parenting, but what are the benefits?*

ANSWER. The first benefit that mother love and father love bring to children is the *difference* itself.

Mothers and fathers parent differently, and this difference provides important diversity in experiences for children. Dr. Pruett explains that fathers have a distinct style of communication and interaction with children. By eight weeks, infants can tell the difference between a male or female interacting with them. Stanford psychologist Eleanor Maccoby, in her book *The Two Sexes,* explains the difference. Mothers are more likely to provide warm, nurturing care for a crying infant.[6] This diversity in itself provides children with a broader, richer experience of contrasting relational interactions—more so than for children who are raised by only one gender. Whether they realize it or not, by sheer experience children are learning at the earliest age that men and women are different and have different ways of dealing with most aspects of life.

---

[2]"Shuttle Diplomacy," *Psychology Today*, July-August 1993, p. 15.

[3]Ronald P. Rohner and Robert A. Veneziano, "The Importance of Father Love: History and Contemporary Evidence," *Review of General Psychology* 5, no. 4 (2001): 382.

[4]Brenda Hunter, *The Power of Mother Love: Transforming Both Mother and Child* (Colorado Springs: Waterbrook, 1997).

[5]Erik Erikson, cited in Kyle D. Pruett, *The Nurturing Father* (New York: Warner Books, 1987), p. 49.

[6]Eleanor E. Maccoby, *The Two Sexes: Growing Up Apart; Coming Together* (Cambridge, Mass.: Harvard University Press, 1999), p. 261.

QUESTION 2. *How do these differences affect children?*

ANSWER. First, mothers and fathers play differently. Fathers tend to *play with* children, and mothers tend to *care for* children. While both mothers and fathers are physical, they are physical in different ways.

Fathers

- tickle and wrestle with their children
- toss their babies in the air
- roughhouse, rather than play house
- stress competition
- encourage independence

Fathers stimulate development of *large* motor skills.

Mothers

- comfort and cuddle their children
- stress equity
- encourage security

Mothers stimulate development of *fine* motor skills.

One study found that 70 percent of father-infant games were more physical and action-oriented while only 4 percent of mother-infant play was.[7]

Fathering expert John Snarey explains that children who roughhouse with their fathers learn that biting, kicking and other forms of physical violence are not acceptable. They learn self-control by being told when "enough is enough" and when to "settle down."[8] Girls and boys both learn a healthy balance between timidity and aggression from moms and dads. Children need mom's softness as well as dad's roughhousing. Both provide security and confidence in their own ways by communicating love and physical intimacy.

Fathers Push Limits, Mothers Encourage Security

Go to any playground, close your eyes and listen to the parents. Who is usually saying, "Be careful," "Not so fast," "Not so high"? And who usually says, "Go for it," "Go higher," "Go faster"? Of course, the fathers are most likely

---

[7]Ibid., p. 266.

[8]John Snarey, cited in David Popenoe, *Life Without Father: Compelling New Evidence That Fatherhood and Marriage Are Indispensable for the Good of Children and Society* (New York: Free Press, 1996), p. 144.

encouraging their children to push limits, to swing a little higher, run further, ride their bikes a little faster, throw the ball a little harder. And mothers are more likely to encourage safety, reserve and playing it safe.

This difference can cause disagreement between mom and dad on what is best for the child. But the difference is essential for children. Either of these parenting styles by themselves can be unhealthy. One can tend toward encouraging risk without consideration of consequences. The other tends to avoid risk, which can fail to build independence, confidence and progress. But joined together, they keep each other in balance and help children remain safe while expanding their experiences and confidence.

QUESTION 3. *I heard of a study that showed how mothers and fathers communicate differently. Does this make a difference?*

ANSWER. Yes. A major study showed that when speaking to children, mothers and fathers tend to be different. Mothers are more likely to simplify their words and speak on the child's level. Most men are not as inclined to modify their language for the child.[9]

Mother's way facilitates immediate communication. Father's way challenges the child to expand his or her vocabulary and linguistic skills, an important building block of academic success.

Father's talk tends to be more brief, directive and to the point. It also makes greater use of subtle body language and facial expressions. Mothers tend to be more descriptive, personal and verbally encouraging. Children who don't have daily exposure to both won't learn how to understand and use both styles of conversation as they grow. These boys and girls will be at a disadvantage because they will experience these different ways of communicating in relationships with teachers, bosses and other authority figures.

QUESTION 4. *What about discipline?*

ANSWER. Yes, there is a very important difference in the ways mothers and fathers discipline their children. Educational psychologist Carol Gilligan tells us that

---

[9]Maccoby, *The Two Sexes*, p. 269.

Fathers stress	Mothers stress
• justice	• sympathy
• fairness	• grace
• duty (based on rules)	• care
Fathers tend to enforce rules sternly and objectively. This teaches children the objectivity and consequences of right and wrong.	• help (based on relationships)
	Mothers tend to enforce rules relative to the situation with grace and sympathy. This provides a sense of hopefulness in the child.

Again, either of these by themselves is not good, but together they create a healthy, proper balance.

QUESTION 5. *What are other ways the mother-and-father differences matter?*

ANSWER. *Fathers and mothers prepare children for life differently.* Dads tend to see their children in relation to the rest of the world. Mothers tend to see the rest of the world in relation to their children. Think about it.

What motivates most mothers as parents? They are motivated primarily by things from the outside world that could hurt their child (for example, lightning, accidents, disease, strange people, dogs or cats, etc.). Fathers, while not unconcerned with these things, tend to focus on how their children will or will not be prepared for something they might encounter in the world (for example, a bully, being nervous around the opposite sex, baseball or soccer tryouts, etc.).

Fathers tend toward helping children see that particular attitudes and behaviors have certain consequences. For instance, fathers are more likely to tell their children that if they aren't nice to others, kids won't want to play with them. Or if they don't do well in school, they won't get into a good college or land a good job. Mothers are more likely to try to soften the blows of these life realities on their children. Fathers are more likely to help children prepare for the reality and harshness of the real world, building confidence and problem-solving skills. Mothers are more inclined to help protect and comfort against the world, offering security.

This truth was unwittingly demonstrated in a profile of a lesbian family recently in *USA Today*. The article featured a lesbian couple, their male sperm donor and his gay partner. They all consider themselves a family. They have one three-year-old boy and are pregnant with another son. The article observes that there is occasional head-butting between the adults on how to raise the child. The biological father thinks the women "pamper Alec too much." He explains, "When he falls down, she wants to rush over and make sure he is OK. I know he will be fine." But the father says he defers to the women, who are the legal parents.[10] Unfortunately this child is not getting the benefit of his father because of the kind of life the adults desire.

QUESTION 6. *Wouldn't fathers help children understand the world of men, and mothers the world of women?*

ANSWER. Exactly. Men and women are different. They tend to eat differently. They dress differently. They smell different. They groom themselves differently. They often cope with life differently. Fathers do "man things," and women do "lady things."

Both mothers and fathers help little girls grow to be women and little boys to be men. Anthropologist Suzanne Frayser explains this is constant in all human societies: "Each process complements the other. The boy can look at his father and see what he should do to be a male; he can look at his mother and see what he should *not* do to be a male." Frayser continues, "The importance of contrasts in gender roles and specification of gender identity may be clues to the *psychological importance of sexual differentiation in all societies.*"[11] Girls and boys who grow up with a father are more familiar and secure with the curious world of men.

Girls who are close to their fathers

• have healthier relationships with boys in adolescence and men in adult-

---

[10]Karen Peterson, "Looking Straight at Gay Parents," *USA Today*, March 10, 2004, 2D.
[11]Suzanne G. Frayser, *Varieties of Sexual Experience: Anthropological Perspective on Human Sexuality* (New York: Human Relations Area File Press, 1985), p. 86 (emphasis added).

hood. This is because they learn from their fathers how proper men act.

- have a healthy familiarity with the world of men. They don't wonder how a man's facial stubble feels, or how it feels to be hugged by strong arms.

This knowledge builds emotional security and safety from the exploitation of predatory males.

Boys who are close to their fathers

- are more secure in their masculinity and less likely to be violent.
- have their masculinity affirmed and learn from their fathers how to channel their maleness and strength in positive ways.

Fathers help boys and girls understand proper male sexuality, hygiene, behavior and work in age-appropriate ways.

Mothers help boys understand the female world and develop a sensitivity toward women. They also help boys know how to relate and communicate with women.

QUESTION 7. *How do mothers and fathers help children interact respectfully with the opposite sex?*

ANSWER. A married father is substantially less likely to abuse his wife or children than men in any other category.[12] This means that boys and girls with married fathers learn by observation how men should treat women.

Girls with involved fathers, therefore, are more likely to select for themselves good husbands because they have a proper standard by which to judge all candidates. Fathers themselves also help weed out bad candidates. Boys raised with fathers are more likely to be good husbands because they can emulate their fathers' successes and learn from their failures. This is per-

---

[12]Jan Stets and Murray A. Strauss, "The Marriage License as a Hitting License: A Comparison of Assaults in Dating, Cohabiting, and Married Couples," *Journal of Family Violence* 4 (1989): 161-80; Jan Stets, "Cohabiting and Marital Aggression: The Role of Social Isolation," *Journal of Marriage and the Family* 53 (1991): 669-80; Michael Gordon, "The Family Environment of Sexual Abuse: A Comparison of Natal and Stepfather Abuse," *Child Abuse and Neglect* 13 (1985): 121-30; Michael Stiffman et al., "Household Composition and Risk of Fatal Child Maltreatment," *Pediatrics* 109 (2002): 615-21; Frank Putnam, "Ten Year Research Update Review: Child Sexual Abuse," *Journal of the American Academy of Child and Adolescent Psychiatry* 42 (2003): 269-79.

haps why societies with involved fathers are more likely to be female-affirming cultures.[13]

Girls and boys with married mothers learn from their mothers what healthy and respectful female relationships with men look like. Girls who observe their mothers confidently and lovingly interacting with their fathers learn how to interact confidently with men. Same-sex homes can't provide this important example and therefore will have a difficult time helping their children have healthy heterosexual relationships.

CONCLUSION

Mothers and fathers matter in many vital ways. The truths we have just observed inform Dr. David Popenoe's warning against saying that children only need loving parents:

> We should disavow the notion that "mommies can make good daddies," just as we should disavow the popular notion of radical feminists that "daddies can make good mommies." . . . The two sexes are different to the core, and each is necessary—culturally and biologically—for the optimal development of a human being.[14]

Those concerned with proper child development want children to have daily access to the different and complementary ways mothers and fathers parent. The same-sex marriage and parenting proponents say this doesn't matter and that biological parents don't necessarily have a responsibility to their children. They are wrong, and their lack of understanding will hurt children. Children growing up in intentionally mother-only or father-only homes will suffer in terms of lack of confidence, independence and security. Boys and girls will be at greater risk for gender confusion, abuse and exploitation from other men. They will be less likely to have healthy respect for both women and men as they grow into adult-

---

[13]Scott Coltrane, "Father-Child Relationships and the Status of Women: A Cross-Cultural Study," *American Journal of Sociology* 93 (1988): 1088.

[14]David Popenoe, *Life Without Father: Compelling New Evidence That Fatherhood and Marriage Are Indispensable for the Good of Children and Society* (New York: Free Press, 1996), p. 197.

hood. This research shows us it is actually unloving to say that children just need two loving parents. They need a mother and father, and to intentionally deny them either is cruel.

11

How Heterosexuals Paved the Way for the Same-Sex Family

There are a few fundamental qualities of marriage, and these are found in *every* human civilization. It's important to think about and understand these qualities.

All societies recognize that

- Marriage regulates sexual relationships between men and women.
- Marriage is a durable union, lasting for life, or at least (in other societies) as long as the child is developing into young adulthood.
- Marriage is always between men and women.
- Marriage is always about the next generation.

We find these qualities running consistently through all cultures since the dawn of humanity. However, American culture, in the last thirty to forty years, has challenged some of the most fundamental parts of marriage.

It's important to remind ourselves that homosexuals aren't the only group challenging the meaning of marriage. Heterosexuals too have been busy at this for many decades, and the results have been dramatically harmful to human well-being. We need to recognize and understand this.

QUESTION 1. *How have heterosexuals challenged the core definition of marriage?*

ANSWER. In many ways, actually. But many of these challenges are not widely recognized or appreciated.

First, a major redefinition of marriage occurred with the growth of our culture of contraception. The emergence of widespread contraception, especially the emergence of the pill, helped separate sexuality and marriage from childbearing. While many people use contraception in order to plan good, healthy families, it also encouraged a cavalier attitude toward children among many others: "If you want children, that's fine. If you don't, that's fine too." "Sex does not have to be about the possibility of babies," a contracepting culture told us.

Concurrent with this development, our society began to believe that when a woman didn't want a child (for whatever reason) and she got pregnant, she should have the option of stopping the pregnancy. As a result, abortion became more widespread than most are comfortable with. Abortion obliterates the very understanding of parenting as well as the human social contract so we are no longer obliged to care for the weakest among us. Some lives are expendable based on whether or not they are wanted. For the first time parenthood didn't demand protection of a child but rather allowed for the child's destruction. But thousands of women have found it easier to remove a baby from the womb than from their heart. They grieve deeply at the loss of their child, becoming the secondary victim of an abortion culture.

But abortion law did something more than corrupt the parent-child relationship. It changed the definition of marriage. It corrupted the mutuality of the husband-wife relationship. It says a wife can destroy a growing life in her womb, and the husband, the father of the child, is disallowed from serving as his child's protector. According to the law the woman has the unilateral choice of whether to bring the baby to term or end the young life. Dad has no role as a parent in this process—and thus he becomes a nonparent. This sets husband and wife against each other.

With children optional, parenthood is determined not by biology but mere declaration. We are not parents because biology brings us to that point but merely because we *want* (or *don't* want) to be parents. When intention rather than biology is the driving criteria for *who* becomes a parent and *when,* then a culture can legitimize same-sex couples who can't become parents biologically but only by a declarative statement of will. Becoming parents by will rather than biology further cements the growing idea that parents (regardless of orientation) need not be responsible for their offspring. Their

DNA may be in the new child, but if their heart is not in it, why should they feel any responsibility?

Likewise, marriage itself is reduced to the thinnest possible dimension: a private, expressive, emotional relationship between two people. This shallow understanding of marriage is being latched onto by the same-sex marriage proponents and used to make their case for redefining marriage: "If marriage is about two people loving each other and committing themselves to each other, why can't we?" Gender gets lost. *But marriage is much more than people who are in love.* It's about much more than adults. It links couples with the creation of children and the healthy, safe development of the next generation.

Second, the sexual revolution proclaimed that sexual mores were not needed. In fact, the sex revolutionaries claimed that sexual regulation was detrimental. So we divorced sexuality from marriage, thinking this would enhance the experience, but instead the opposite was true. Untethered sexuality left more people with greater sexual frustration, life-threatening disease, dysfunction and an epidemic of broken lives. Early pioneer of sociology Pitirim Sorokin was correct when he predicted in the mid-1950s a sexual revolution would "destroy the real freedom of normal love; and in lieu of enriching and ennobling the sexual passion, it reduces it to mere copulation."[1] The sexual revolution also gave us a culture of abortion that separated parent and child. Again, children became optional in the ultimate sense.

Third, the divorce revolution proclaimed that the "till death do us part" vow of marriage was optional. This revolution was built on the idea that we could exit bad marriages for better ones whenever we want and everything would work out well. In fact, it was believed that happier adults in better relationships would produce better, happier children. So it nearly became a duty for people to leave so-so marriages to find better ones. But things didn't work out well. In fact, the divorce revolution actually worked out far worse for both children and adults than anyone ever imagined.

The blessing of children. Sexual regulation. Lifelong commitment in

---

[1]Pitirim A. Sorokin, *The American Sex Revolution* (Boston: Porter Sargent, 1956), p. 88.

marriage. The loss of these three crucial ideals has diminished our humanity. They have brought levels of abortion on demand far too high for even the most liberal among us. The loss has brought us rampant sexually transmitted diseases, sexual frustration, dysfunction, gender confusion and a greater objectification of women. The loss has brought us shattered childhoods and anxious, broken adults. Experience clearly proclaims that when we tamper with any of the fundamental qualities of marriage, bad things happen to people. Our love for others demands that we try our best to limit such changes in family and society to spare more people from harm.

QUESTION 2. *But all of this shows how heterosexuals have messed up marriage, what does it have to do with same-sex marriage?*

ANSWER. Homosexual activists are writing the next chapter of marriage-tinkering, and they are challenging the last fundamental quality of marriage: "husband *and* wife." They want us to believe that male and female—mothers and fathers—don't matter for the family.

Do we really believe we won't have the same sorts of deep and unforeseen problems with this experiment? Are we such slow learners? You'd think we would know by now to resist such tinkering. But still, some in our society push change for no other reason than they want to structure their lives in certain ways, and they demand all of us buy into it. The result is that children will be forced into another experiment with the family.

QUESTION 3. *Why does marriage provide rich benefits that other relationships don't?*

ANSWER. First, we must recognize that the kind of rich benefits marriage provides aren't found in cohabiting relationships, even long-term committed ones. Compared to their married peers, cohabiters consistently have lower rates of well-being than married people.[2] Why? Because cohabiting relationships are ambiguous. Usually each partner has a different understand-

---

[2]Linda J. Waite, "Trends in Men's and Women's Well-Being in Marriage," in *The Ties That Bind: Perspectives on Marriage and Cohabitation*, ed. Linda J. Waite (Hawthorne, N.Y.: Aldine de Gruyter, 2000), p. 386.

ing of the nature and future of the relationship.[3] In marriage the couple is clear about the claim they have on each other. Husbands are more likely to come home after work and not stay out all night with the guys than boyfriends are. Wives and husbands are not as likely to flirt with others outside the relationship. Marriage helps them know who they belong to emotionally and sexually.

Marriage provides commitment and relational clarity, not only for the couple but for the extended family and the community as well. In marriage everyone knows what the nature of the relationship is. They don't have to guess or wonder behind the couple's back. And this commitment and clarity is what helps the couple and the surrounding community make the kind of contributions to each other that lend themselves to increased well-being. Cohabiting relationships do not do this.

Children also make positive contributions to marriage. Children (and spouses) help individuals live outside of their own interests. Children require us to sacrifice for and commit ourselves to work for the good of others. This can cause some stress in marriage (yes, raising kids can be stressful!), but it is also a source of great joy and satisfaction.[4] Parents try harder to do well and succeed at work. They strive to improve their ability to provide for their family by securing higher levels of education and promotions at work. They avoid risky behaviors. Parents take better care of themselves because they know children are depending on them. Married parents also have each other to help take care of themselves. They can help shoulder the work required in raising children. And children help adults be more responsible.

Of course, same-sex partners can commit to each other, even though research shows they are less successful at sustaining long-term relationships than heterosexuals. They can also raise children. So neither of these qualities that make marriage beneficial are exclusive to heterosexuals. But there is an important quality of heterosexual marriage that is exclusive to it.

---

[3]Larry Bumpass, James A. Sweet and Andrew Cherlin, "The Role of Cohabitation in Declining Rates of Marriage," *Journal of Marriage and the Family* 53 (1991): 913-27.
[4]Jean M. Twenge et al., "Parenthood and Marital Satisfaction: A Meta-Analytic Review," *Journal of Marriage and the Family* 65 (2003): 574-83.

QUESTION 4. *Why does the male-female nature of marriage matter?*

ANSWER. Marriage brings different things together. Recently, I (Glenn) was at a meeting in Manhattan with a very interesting group of scholars and community reformers. We were at this meeting because we are all interested in developing a movement to recover a culture of marriage. People from all walks of life, political persuasions and religious ideologies were there. Someone in the room recognized this remarkable diversity and described the gathering as "a marriage of people concerned about marriage." It would have been foolish to describe this cooperative effort as a "marriage" if we were all from the same mind or political spin. But because our differences complemented each other and the work we were doing, she was right to describe it as a marriage.

Marriages don't bring similar things together. They bring different things together and help them work for a common good. Same-sex unions are not marriage because they don't bring the two different parts of humanity together. They bring *similar* things together, thus the word *same* in "same-sex marriage."

Marriage is beneficial for men, women and children because it brings men and women together into a lifelong, committed, cooperative relationship. It is a simple yet remarkably profound human dynamic.

Women complete men, and men complete women. The way that men and women complete and complement each other is rooted in their God-given differences. A man can't complete another man, nor can a woman complete another woman. They can have warm, loving relationships to be sure. Few would deny this. But they can't complete one another. They have very little in their sex-based similarities to offer each other. That is why marriage in all human civilizations is heterosexual; it brings together the two necessary parts of humanity. Same-sex relationships can't provide the many dynamics humanity needs to live well and produce the next generation.

To get an idea of how men and women complement one another and create a fuller life than either sex can create on its own, think of your workplace or place of worship. What would these places look like if they only consisted of men? What if they only consisted of women? How different would they be? How would the absence of the other gender impoverish your work or worship? For the same-sex marriage proposition to be reasonable, we would have to say this doesn't matter. But of course we know it does. It's undeniable.

Ponder how deeply this absence would be felt in the smallness and intimacy of a family. For there is no other institution in any society that so effectively brings together male and female into a cooperative relationship at such a deep and profound level. Yes, churches, corporations and civic clubs bring men and women together, but not as deeply and intimately as marriage does. None of these institutions creates a "one flesh" union like marriage does. *And this coming together of the two parts of humanity is what provides the rich positive benefits of marriage for adults, children and society.* This is true in both civil and religious marriages. Marriage as an institutional entity, whether legal or religious, is not what creates these collective benefits. Males and females create them when they cooperate together in exclusive, committed, self-sacrificing relationships. This is how humanity is constructed, and this is how we thrive. Law and religion recognize and celebrate the benefits in special and unique ways. As anthropologist of sexuality Suzanne Frayser explains, social "differentiation [between male and female] is important for the survival of the group, the psychological stability of the individual, and the maintenance of the social order."[5] In short, male and female matter far more than we realize, in far deeper ways.

Just as it is wrong to say children are optional, sex should be set free from marriage and marriage need not be for life, it is wrong to say that husband or wife, mother or father don't matter for the family. We diminish the significance of male and female at our own peril. To do so denies our very humanity.

---

[5]Suzanne G. Frayser, *Varieties of Sexual Experience: Anthropological Perspective on Human Sexuality* (New York: Human Relations Area File Press, 1985), pp. 89-90.

CONCLUSION

Marriage provides real and important health and well-being benefits for adults and children because of the unique qualities of marriage. The primary quality of marriage that provides these benefits is the way it brings men and women together into long-term, exclusive, cooperative and complementary relationships. Marriage is beneficial in the way it makes the two parts of humanity one. The way male and female complete each other helps us live in the trueness of our humanity. Same-sex relationships deny our humanity.

CHEAT SHEET FOR SECTION II
Healthy marriage provides rich benefits for . . .

1. adults by way of

increasing

- general happiness and contentedness
- all measures of physical and mental health
- healthy, longer lifespan
- sexual fulfillment
- work dependability and productivity
- financial earning and saving power
- satisfaction and success in parenting

decreasing

- depression, alcoholism and other substance abuses
- overall life stress
- domestic violence

2. children by way of

increasing

- all levels of intellectual and educational development
- all levels of physical and emotional health
- sympathy and consideration of others

decreasing

- the need to visit doctors for physical and emotional problems
- incidents of idleness (being out of school and not working)
- being in trouble at school or with the law
- participation in drugs, violence, and premarital sex and childbearing
- the danger of physical and sexual violence
- the likelihood of living in poverty

Children need mothers and fathers because

- mothers and fathers parent differently
- mothers and fathers play differently
- fathers push limits; mothers stress safety
- mothers and fathers communicate differently
- mothers and fathers discipline differently
- mothers and fathers help children prepare for life and the world differently
- mothers and fathers provide a unique look at the world of women and men
- fathers teach respect for women, and mothers and fathers teach respect for relationship

WHY DOES MARRIAGE PROVIDE THESE BENEFITS?

1. The commitment and clarity of marriage is what helps the couple and the surrounding community make the kind of contributions to each other that lend themselves to increased well-being. Cohabiting relationships are not as good at doing this.

2. Children also make positive contributions to marriage. Children require us to sacrifice for and commit ourselves to work for the good of others. Parents work harder to do well and succeed at work; they avoid risky behavior and take better care of themselves.

3. Married males and females complete each other by cooperating together. And this coming together of the two parts of humanity is what provides the rich, positive benefits of marriage for adults, children and society.

Same-sex unions and parenting cannot bring this completion. They are by definition always lacking a necessary part of humanity. Therefore they can't do what humanity needs them to do: raise a healthy next generation of humanity.

DEBUNKING THE MYTHS ABOUT HOMOSEXUALITY

What causes homosexuality? Are people "born gay"? Is homosexuality simply a normal human variation or a human disorder? Can sexual orientation be changed through therapy?

Today, in the midst of the same-sex marriage debate, many Americans are struggling with these questions. Unfortunately, accurate information about homosexuality is difficult to obtain and misinformation abounds. Fraudulent "facts" about sexual orientation are regularly tossed around by the mainstream media, the corporate world, the halls of academia—even the church. Sadly, many gays and lesbians *themselves* are being "kept in the dark" about the true nature of homosexuality. They're being sold lies: that their sexual orientation is inborn, unchangeable, even a "gift from God." Deception is never compassionate. Lack of understanding is never helpful.

In the section that follows we will examine four of the most common "myths" about homosexuality:

• Homosexuals are "born gay."

• Homosexuality is "normal and natural."

• Homosexuals can't change their sexual orientation.

• All homosexuals want same-sex marriage.

Many Americans have bought into these myths and are unaware that each of them is completely contradicted by scientific research. We'll also look behind these myths and attempt to determine why so many of us (including gays and lesbians) accept them as true.

12

ARE HOMOSEXUALS "BORN GAY"?

Appearing on MSNBC's *Hardball*, Elizabeth Birch, former executive director of the nation's largest gay activist organization, the Human Rights Campaign, discussed the origins of homosexuality with host Chris Matthews. Birch explained that "well-grounded, credible studies have shown that it is likely—highly likely—that [homosexuality] is actually grounded in biology."[1] Matthews smiled and nodded in agreement. But Birch's claim was completely false. *The truth is there are no replicated scientific studies that prove that homosexuality is determined by biological or genetic factors.* Even respected *gay* researchers don't dispute this.

Gay groups such as the Human Rights Campaign (HRC), the Gay and Lesbian Alliance Against Defamation (GLAAD), and the Gay, Lesbian, Straight Education Network (GLSEN) regularly promulgate the myth that homosexuality is genetic. After all, you and I are much more likely to be sympathetic toward homosexual behavior if we believe it is "hard-wired" into human beings. Gay activists have made incredible advances by equating sexual orientation with skin color, comparing their "struggle for equality" with the very real struggle faced by African Americans. Proponents of gay theology have effectively used the "born gay" argument to convince the leadership of several mainline Protestant denominations that homosexuality is "a gift from God."[2]

The myth that homosexuals are born gay is rooted in several groundbreaking research studies published in the early 1990s. Initially, each of

---

[1]Elizabeth Birch, *Hardball with Chris Matthews*, CNBC-TV, May 9, 2001.
[2]See Joe Dallas, *A Strong Delusion: Confronting the "Gay Christian" Movement* (Eugene, Ore.: Harvest House, 1996).

these studies appeared to indicate that homosexuality might have a genetic basis. This research on the possible biological origins of homosexuality created a huge stir in the media at the time. Several major U.S. newsmagazines claimed that scientists might have found a "gay gene."[3]

QUESTION 1. *Can you identify these studies?*

ANSWER. Here's a brief summary of three of the most significant studies claiming to establish a link between a homosexual orientation and biology.

In 1991 Dr. Simon LeVay, a neuroscientist at the Salk Institute in La Jolla, California, examined a specific region of the brain structure called the hypothalamus in deceased homosexual and heterosexual men (medical cadavers). LeVay purportedly discovered that this region was smaller in the brains of gay men, leading him to conclude that this difference might be responsible for the development of homosexuality.[4] In fact, he told *Newsweek* magazine that after the death of his gay lover, he resolved to find a genetic cause for homosexuality or give up scientific research altogether.[5]

That same year psychologist Michael Bailey of Northwestern University (who is sympathetic to gay politics) and psychiatrist Richard Pillard of Boston University School of Medicine (who identifies himself as gay) conducted research on pairs of identical twins. They were attempting to determine if homosexuality might be an inherited trait. Their research appeared to indicate a much higher incidence of homosexuality among male identical twins than among fraternal and nontwin brothers, leading them to postulate a genetic cause for homosexuality.[6]

In 1993 Dr. Dean Hamer of the National Cancer Institute (who also identifies himself as gay) examined genetic material on the X chromosome of nonidentical twin gay brothers. He found that many of these brothers shared a common genetic marker, leading him to conclude that

[3]For example, Larry Thompson, "Search for a Gay Gene," *Time,* June 12, 1995; and "Is This Child Gay?" *Newsweek,* September 9, 1991.
[4]Simon LeVay, "A Difference in the Hypothalamic Structure Between Heterosexual and Homosexual Men," *Science* 253 (1991): 1034-37.
[5]Simon LeVay, cited in "Is This Child Gay?" *Newsweek,* September 9, 1991, p. 52.
[6]J. Michael Bailey and Richard C. Pillard, "A Genetic Study of Male Sexual Orientation," *Archives of General Psychiatry* 48 (1991): 1081-96.

homosexuality must be an inherited trait.[7]

In recent years the research conducted by LeVay, Bailey and Pillard, and Hamer has been criticized on numerous methodological grounds.[8] For example, it turns out that LeVay wasn't certain if the deceased men whose brains he studied were actually heterosexual or homosexual. (Six of the supposedly "straight" men had died of AIDS.) Bailey's twin study was compromised due to "sample bias." (He found his gay twin subjects by advertising in gay magazines.) And the statistical methods he used may have led him to report exaggerated results. Hamer's study actually found several gay men who did *not* have the genetic marker that supposedly contributed to homosexuality. He also found several men who *had* the marker but were not gay. Perhaps even more significantly, other researchers have been unable to replicate the results of any of these studies.[9]

Although you're not likely to read about it in major news outlets like the *New York Times* or hear about it on the *CBS Evening News,* LeVay, Bailey and Pillard, and Hamer have all stated that their studies *did not* prove that homosexuality is genetically or biologically determined. Simon LeVay says, "It's important to stress what I didn't find. I did not prove that homosexuality was genetic, or find a genetic cause for being gay. I didn't show that gay men are born that way, the most common mistake people make in interpreting my work."[10] Dean Hamer notes, "Homosexuality is not purely genetic. . . . [E]nvironmental factors play a role. There is not a single master gene that makes people gay. . . . I don't think we will ever be able to predict who will be gay."[11] And Michael Bailey (who did follow-up research that failed to rep-

---

[7]Stella Hu et al., "Linkage Between Sexual Orientation and Chromosome Xq28 in Males but Not in Females," *Nature Genetics* 11 (1995): 248-56.

[8]For a complete review of these critiques, see Stanton L Jones and Mark A. Yarhouse, *Homosexuality: The Use of Scientific Research in the Church's Moral Debate* (Downers Grove, Ill.: InterVarsity Press, 2000), pp. 60-91.

[9]William Byne and Bruce Parsons, "Human Sexual Orientation: The Biologic Theories Reappraised," *Archives of General Psychiatry* 50 (1993): 228-39; Georgy Rice et al., "Male Homosexuality: Absence of Linkage to Microsatellite Markers at Xq28," *Science* 284 (1999): 665-67.

[10]Simon LeVay, cited in David Nimmons, "Sex and the Brain," *Discover* 15, no. 3 (1994): 64-71.

[11]Dean Hamer, cited in Nancy Mitchell, "Genetics, Sexuality Linked, Study Says," *The [Ogden, Utah] Standard Examiner,* April 30, 1995, p. 7-B.

licate the results of his earlier study) now claims his work "did not provide statistically significant support for the importance of genetic factors" for homosexual orientation.[12]

QUESTION 2. *So what does cause homosexuality?*

ANSWER. It should be remembered that prior to the search for a gay gene, most research on the origins of homosexuality focused on *environmental* factors, such as family dynamics or early sexual abuse.[13]

For example, Irving Bieber and his colleagues found a "triangular" pattern in the family backgrounds of many male homosexuals. These men reported an emotionally detached or hostile father and an enmeshed, "close-binding" mother who tended to "minimize" her husband.[14] Marvin Siegelman found a similar dynamic when he compared the families of 307 homosexuals with a control group of 138 heterosexuals. He stated that

> The homosexuals, in contrast to the heterosexuals, reported their fathers to be more rejecting and less loving. The homosexuals also described their mothers as more rejecting and less loving. . . . [T]he homosexuals indicated less closeness to their fathers than the heterosexuals.[15]

Childhood sexual abuse may also be a factor in the development of homosexuality for some individuals. In the most comprehensive study of human sexuality in America to date, Edward Laumann and his research team found that men and women who had experienced sexual abuse as children were more than three times as likely to report a homosexual orientation as adults.[16] In a study of adolescent boys who had been victims of sexual abuse, researchers Diane Shrier and Robert Johnson found that 58 percent

---

[12]J. Michael Bailey, Michael P. Dunne and Nicholas G. Martin, "Genetic and Environmental Influences on Sexual Orientation and Its Correlates in an Australian Twin Sample," *Journal of Personality and Social Psychology* 78 (2000): 534.

[13]See Jones and Yarhouse, *Homosexuality*.

[14]Irving Bieber et al., *Homosexuality: A Psychoanalytic Study of Male Homosexuals* (New York: Basic Books, 1962), pp. 84-86.

[15]Marvin Siegelman, "Parental Background of Male Homosexuals and Heterosexuals," *Archives of Sexual Behavior* 3 (1974): 10.

[16]Edward Laumann et al., *The Social Organization of Sexuality: Sexual Practices in the United States* (Chicago: University of Chicago Press, 1994), p. 344.

of the boys who had been sexually abused described themselves as either homosexual or bisexual. In contrast, 90 percent of the teen boys who had *not* been abused described themselves as heterosexual.[17]

These days it's not politically correct to talk about family dysfunction or childhood sexual abuse when discussing the possible causes of homosexuality. You will rarely hear these factors discussed in the media, academia or even professional mental health circles. It's likely that such discussion would be branded "intolerant" or "insensitive." Also gay leaders realized years ago that Americans would be much more sympathetic to their arguments for civil rights (including same-sex marriage) if they believed that homosexuality is simply a "normal inborn variation," like eye color.[18]

So, if you consider yourself a thoughtful, caring person and you learn that a gay or lesbian coworker wasn't "born gay" but instead may have been adversely affected by unhealthy family dynamics or childhood sexual abuse, how should you respond? Gay groups celebrate homosexual orientation with "gay pride" parades, and many liberal denominations claim that homosexuality is a "gift from God." But we must ask ourselves this: if a gay friend's homosexual orientation might be due to negative circumstances in his or her childhood, shouldn't our natural response be one of *compassion* rather than celebration?

The current consensus in the scientific community is that there is absolutely no proof that people are born gay. Instead, homosexuality is likely caused by a host of interacting factors. Columbia University professors Richard Friedman and Jennifer Downey sum up the state of the research:

> At clinical conferences one often hears that homosexual orientation is fixed and unmodifiable. Neither assertion is true. . . . [T]he assertion that homosexuality is genetic is so reductionistic that it must be dismissed out of hand as a general principle of psychology. . . . What

---

[17]Diane Shrier and Robert L. Johnson, "Sexual Victimization of Boys: An Ongoing Study of an Adolescent Medicine Clinic Population," *Journal of the National Medical Association* 80 (1988): 1189-93, cited in Jones and Yarhouse, *Homosexuality*, p. 57.

[18]Marshall Kirk and Hunter Madsen, *After the Ball: How America Will Conquer Its Fear and Hatred of Gays in the 90s* (New York: Doubleday, 1989).

causes homosexuality? It is apparent that biological, psychological
and social factors interacting in complex and various ways shape human sexual orientation.[19]

Lesbian author Dr. Camille Paglia is more blunt in her assessment:

Homosexuality is not normal. On the contrary it is a challenge to the
norm. . . . Nature exists whether academics like it or not. And in nature, procreation is the single relentless rule. That is the norm. Our
sexual bodies were designed for reproduction. . . . No one is born gay.
The idea is ridiculous. . . . [H]omosexuality is an adaptation, not an
inborn trait.[20]

Paglia's statement is striking; she dares to suggest that homosexuality is
neither normal nor natural. She would say that one of its defining virtues is
that it challenges nature and convention. But gay organizations are working
hard to convince us that homosexuality is "just like" heterosexuality. Is it?
Or does recent psychological research paint a different picture? We will explore that in our next chapter.

CONCLUSION

Contrary to what many Americans believe, there are no replicated scientific studies demonstrating that homosexuality is determined by biological
or genetic factors. In the early 1990s, several research studies appeared to
support a biological cause for homosexual attraction. However, none of
those studies has been duplicated, and each suffered from serious methodological flaws. The gay-sympathetic scientists who conducted the studies now admit the limitations of their work and have stated that there is no
reliable evidence that homosexuals are born gay. Other research has sug-
gested a possible correlation between homosexuality and family dynamics
and early sexual abuse. The current consensus among leading researchers
is that homosexuality is likely caused by a complex host of interacting bi-

[19]Richard C. Friedman and Jennifer I. Downey, *Sexual Orientation and Psychoanalysis: Sexual Science and Clinical Practice* (New York: Columbia University Press, 2002), p. 39.
[20]Camille Paglia, *Vamps and Tramps* (New York: Vintage Books, 1994), pp. 70-72.

ological, psychological and social factors. Although there is little scientific support for the "born gay" theory, the major gay organizations continue to claim that homosexuality is innate and biologically determined. In many cases the media helps to perpetuate this myth through inaccurate or uncritical news reporting.

13

Is Homosexuality
"Normal and Natural"?

Brian, a fourteen-year-old high school freshman, is struggling with feelings of sexual confusion. An artistic, sensitive boy, he has never felt accepted by his father, a "tough as nails" military officer who favors Brian's older brother, a star athlete. Ever since he can remember, Brian has identified much more with his mother, a woman who is unhappy in her marriage and looks to Brian for emotional support as her "special confidant." Brian finds he is much more comfortable engaging in more "feminine" activities with his mother, like cooking and shopping for clothes. It is where he feels "like himself." He also feels rejected by his male classmates, some of whom deride him with labels like "sissy" and "queerboy." One particularly mean boy consistently calls him "faggot" in place of his first name. He tries to pretend it doesn't hurt, but of course it wounds him deeply.

A few months ago Brian began attending his high school's Gay-Straight Alliance club, an "outreach" program sponsored by a national gay organization called The Gay, Lesbian, Straight Education Network (GLSEN). Brian's history teacher is the faculty adviser to the club, and he invited Brian to attend. At the Gay-Straight Alliance meetings Brian was told that homosexuality is normal, natural and "genetic." He also learned about various "support groups" in the community for homosexual, bisexual, transgender and "questioning" youth.[1]

At one of the community support group meetings, Brian was invited to a party hosted by several gay male college students. These men served margaritas and wine coolers to the high school kids who attended, including

---

[1]Much of GLSEN's curriculum can be accessed at <www.glsen.org>.

Brian. Brian had too much to drink and a twenty-two-year-old man named Tony took advantage of him sexually. Scared and confused after the experience, Brian now wonders if he might be gay.

Searching for answers on the Internet, Brian finds the website for the Human Rights Campaign (HRC), the nation's most powerful gay activist organization. A few clicks take him to the HRC's *Resource Guide to Coming Out*. This is what Brian reads:

> Being Gay, Lesbian, Bisexual or Transgender Is Natural.
>
> . . . The fact is same-sex love and gender variance has occurred throughout history, in every nation and culture. They are natural variations among humans, and may have occurred somewhere in your own family's history. When people say being GLBT is unnatural, they mean it is against their preconceived idea of, or conditioned assumptions about, what is natural. . . .
>
> Just remember: The anxiety you are feeling is primarily the result of family or social prejudice against GLBT people.[2]

QUESTION 1. *Brian is in a hard place. What does he need to know?*

ANSWER. First he should be told what we learned in chapter twelve: homosexuality is not genetic. He should also learn that homosexual behavior is not good for him. But HRC's *Resource Guide to Coming Out* won't tell him the truth, that kids who experiment with homosexual behavior are significantly more likely to engage in a variety of other high-risk behaviors such as

- marijuana and cocaine use before the age thirteen
- sexual intercourse before the age thirteen
- sexual intercourse with four or more partners
- sexual contact against one's will[3]

As they encourage him to "come out," the people at the Human Rights

---

[2]"Resource Guide to Coming Out," Human Rights Campaign Foundation, <www.hrc.org/Content/NavigationMenu/Coming_Out/Get_Informed4/Resources2/Resource_Guide_to_Coming_Out/The_Facts_About_Sexuality_and_Gender_Identity.htm>.

[3]Robert Garofalo et al., "The Association Between Health Risk Behaviors and Sexual Orientation Among a School-based Sample of Adolescents," *Pediatrics* 101 (1998): 895-902.

Campaign won't tell Brian what lies ahead for him if he embraces a homosexual identity. They won't let him know that homosexuals are more likely to suffer from mental illness, alcohol and substance abuse, and a variety of life-threatening diseases such as AIDS, certain types of cancer, and hepatitis.[4] They won't inform him that, on average, male homosexuals die a premature death by up to twenty years.[5] And they neglect to mention that both gays and lesbians are more likely than heterosexuals to commit suicide, and to be victims of domestic violence at the hands of a sex partner.[6]

Gay activist organizations like HRC, GLSEN and GLAAD have made great strides in convincing heterosexual Americans that homosexuality is "perfectly normal." So even though the medical and psychiatric evidence demonstrates that there are numerous risk factors associated with homosexuality, you and I (and kids like Brian) rarely hear that side of the story. It's unlikely that topics such as depression, anal cancer or higher rates of gay domestic abuse will be discussed on TV programs like *Will & Grace, Queer Eye for the Straight Guy* or *Boy Meets Boy.* It's doubtful that you will ever hear the statement Matthew Shepard's mom made regarding her son: "Matt used to say to me, 'Why can't I find anything happy about gay people?'"[7]

QUESTION 2. *What percentage of the population is homosexual?*

ANSWER. About 1 to 2 percent. According to the most comprehensive, scientifically rigorous study of sexual behavior to date, approximately 2 percent of American men and 0.9 percent of American women identify themselves as homosexual. This research, conducted by sociologist Edward

---

[4]W. E. Owen Jr., "Medical Problems of the Homosexual Adolescent," *Journal of Adolescent Health Care* 6, no. 4 (1985): 278-85; Theo G. M. Sandfort et al., "Same-Sex Sexual Behavior and Psychiatric Disorders," *Archives of General Psychiatry* 58 (2001): 85-91.

[5]R. S. Hogg et al., "Modeling the Impact of HIV Disease on Mortality in Gay and Bisexual Men," *International Journal of Epidemiology* 26 (1997): 657-61.

[6]D. M. Fergusson, L. J. Horwood and A. L. Beautrais, "Is Sexual Orientation Related to Mental Health Problems and Suicidality in Young People?" *Archives of General Psychiatry* 56 (1999): 876-80; G. L. Greenwood et al., "Battering Victimization Among a Probability-based Sample of Men Who Have Sex with Men," *American Journal of Public Health* 92 (2002): 1964-69; "Extent, Nature, and Consequences of Intimate Partner Violence," *U.S. Department of Justice: Office of Justice Programs,* July 2000, p. 30.

[7]Cited in John Cloud, "The New Face of Gay Power," *Time,* October 13, 2003, p. 56.

Laumann and his colleagues at the University of Chicago, also found that an additional 0.8 percent of men and 0.5 percent of women identify themselves as bisexual.[8]

Although approximately two out of one hundred Americans are homosexual, gay organizations are prone to "inflate the numbers," claiming that "10 percent" of the population is gay. Bruce Voller, the former chairman of the National Gay Task Force, takes credit for originating the 10 percent figure in the late 1970s. Voller says that he came up with this number in order to convince politicians and the American public that "we [gays and lesbians] are everywhere."[9] The "one in ten" figure also serves another purpose: it supports the notion that homosexuality is "normal."

Even though it is a manufactured statistic, the 10 percent number is frequently quoted by gay advocates in a variety of settings. For example, lesbian educator Virginia Uribe argued for her "Project 10" outreach program to "gay" students in the Los Angeles city schools using the 10 percent figure.[10] In the brochure "I Think I Might Be Gay . . . Now What Do I Do?" the gay youth organization *Out Proud* tells teens, "We know that about one out of ten people in the world is gay or lesbian."[11]

Lesbian activist Jill Harris admits that while gay groups know the 10 percent number is a gross exaggeration, it proves helpful in advocacy efforts: "The thing about the one-in-ten . . . I think people probably always did know it was inflated but it was a nice number that you could point to, that you could say, 'one-in-ten,' and it's a really good way to get people to visualize that we are here."[12]

University of Chicago's Laumann believes that one of the reasons the 10 percent figure may seem reasonable to many people (particularly to gays and lesbians) is that many homosexuals tend to migrate to the nation's largest metropolitan areas, giving rise to the perception that "gays are everywhere."

---

[8]Edward O. Laumann et al., *The Social Organization of Sexuality: Sexual Practices in the United States* (Chicago: University of Chicago Press, 1994), pp. 283-320.

[9]Ibid., p. 289.

[10]*Project 10 Handbook* (Friends of Project 10).

[11]See <http://www.outproud.org/brochure_think_gay.html>. Accessed June 15, 2004.

[12]*Gay Rights/Special Rights* (Jeremiah Films, 1993).

For men living in gay communities in such cities as New York, San Francisco, Los Angeles, or Chicago, this implies that an even higher proportion of the men with whom they come in contact would be gay identified. Research implying that the "true" percentage was on the order of 1 or 2 percent would seem quite inaccurate to such people.[13]

Media coverage of gays and lesbians (including the wide variety of television programs and films featuring gay characters) may also contribute to the belief that the percentage of homosexuals in the population is much greater than it truly is. In fact a Gallup poll conducted in 2002 found that, on average, Americans believe that *one out of five* persons is gay or lesbian.[14]

QUESTION 3. *Haven't mental health organizations said homosexuality is normal?*

ANSWER. Several years ago lesbian author Urvashi Vaid argued that gay activists must "create a society in which homosexuality is regarded as healthy, natural, and normal. . . . [T]hat is the most important agenda item."[15] An important milestone in that agenda was achieved in 1973 when gay activists succeeded in their goal to have homosexuality removed as a "mental disorder" from the American Psychiatric Association's *Diagnostic and Statistical Manual of Mental Disorders,* or DSM. The decision to change the DSM was made under relentless pressure from gay groups, and it caused a huge division within the ranks of America's psychiatrists.[16]

QUESTION 4. *How did the change to the DSM happen?*

ANSWER. In his comprehensive book about this event, *Homosexuality and American Psychiatry: The Politics of Diagnosis,* author Ronald Bayer describes the history of the APA decision. In the original version of the DSM (which was published in 1952), homosexuality was listed as a "sociopathic personality

---

[13]Laumann et al., *Social Organization*, p. 307.

[14]Jennifer Robison, *The Gallup Poll Tuesday Briefing*, October 8, 2002.

[15]Gabriel Rotello, *Sexual Ecology: AIDS and the Destiny of Gay Men* (New York: Penguin, 1997), p. 286.

[16]A detailed description of these events can be found in Jones and Yarhouse, *Homosexuality;* and Joe Dallas, *A Strong Delusion: Confronting the "Gay Christian" Movement* (Eugene, Ore.: Harvest House, 1996).

disturbance." In 1968, the second version of the DSM moved homosexuality from the category of personality disturbance to that of "sexual deviations."[17]

As the gay rights movement gained momentum in the late 1960s and early 1970s, gay activists began protesting at the annual conventions of the American Psychiatric Association (APA) demanding that the organization remove homosexuality from its list of psychiatric conditions. In 1973, after months of negotiations with gay leaders, the APA's board of trustees voted to do just that. Several leading psychiatrists voiced their strong opposition to this decision, so in 1974 the entire membership of the APA was asked to vote on the issue.

Of the APA's ten thousand voting members, almost 40 percent rejected the board's decision to normalize homosexuality. However, the majority ruled, and the condition was removed from the DSM.[18] Dr. Bayer (who is sympathetic to gay causes) admits that the APA decision was based entirely on politics, not science:

> The entire process, from the first confrontation organized by gay demonstrators to the referendum demanded by orthodox psychiatrists, seemed to violate the most basic expectations about how questions of science should be resolved. Instead of being engaged in sober discussion of data, psychiatrists were swept up in a political controversy. The result was not a conclusion based on an approximation of the scientific truth as dictated by reason but was instead an action demanded by the ideological temper of the times.[19]

Even after the vote, the majority of APA members continued to view homosexuality as pathological. Four years after the APA decision, 69 percent of psychiatrists surveyed said they regarded homosexuality as a "pathological adaptation" and 60 percent said they believed that homosexual men were less capable of "mature loving relationships" than heterosexual men.[20] An-

---

[17]Ronald Bayer, *Homosexuality and American Psychiatry: The Politics of Diagnosis* (New York: Basic Books, 1981), pp. 39-40.
[18]Ibid., p. 148.
[19]Ibid., pp. 3-4.
[20]Ibid., p. 167.

other survey, conducted by the APA's Office of International Affairs in 1993, found that almost twenty years after the APA's decision, the majority of psychiatrists around the world continue to believe that homosexuality is a mental illness.[21]

QUESTION 5. *What is the relationship between homosexuality and mental health?*

ANSWER. While the APA no longer officially considers homosexuality a "disorder," recent studies conducted in the United States, New Zealand and the Netherlands indicate that there is a high correlation between homosexual behavior and mental illness.[22] In perhaps the most comprehensive study to date, the *Archives of General Psychiatry* published research that compared the prevalence rates of psychiatric disorders among heterosexuals to the rates among homosexuals. The researchers found that homosexuals (both gays and lesbians) have extremely high rates of psychiatric illness, drug and alcohol abuse, and suicide.[23]

When responding to findings like these, gay activists typically claim that these problems are not due to homosexuality but rather to "intolerance" and a "homophobic society." It is certainly possible that societal pressure could contribute to the emotional difficulties experienced by many homosexuals. But the research cited in the *Archives* was conducted in the Netherlands, which is arguably one of the most gay-friendly countries on the earth. In fact, the authors of the study stated: "the Dutch social climate toward homosexuality has long been and remains considerably more tolerant" than other countries.[24] So it seems unlikely that "social disapproval" is responsible for the high incidence of mental illness and self-destructive behavior reported

---

[21]American Psychiatric Association, "Psychiatrists' Views on Homosexuality," *Psychiatric News*, September 1993.

[22]D. M. Fergusson, L. J. Horwood and A. L. Beautrais, "Is Sexual Orientation Related to Mental Health Problems?" pp. 876-80; R. Herrell et al., "Sexual Orientation and Suicidality: A Co-Twin Control Study in Adult Men," *Archive of General Psychiatry* 56 (1999): 867-74; Theo G. M. Sandfort et al., "Same-Sex Sexual Behavior and Psychiatric Disorders," *Archive of General Psychiatry* 58 (2001): 85-91.

[23]Ibid., pp. 85-91.

[24]Ibid.

by the Dutch researchers. It should be noted that same-sex marriage has been legal in the Netherlands for several years as well.

Researcher Michael Bailey (of the famous "gay-twin studies") believes the new research on homosexuality and mental illness is extremely significant:

> These studies contain arguably the best published data on the association between homosexuality and psychopathology, and both converge on the same unhappy conclusion: homosexual people are at substantially higher risk for some forms of emotional problems, including suicidality, major depression, and anxiety disorder, conduct disorder, and nicotine dependence. . . . The strength of the new studies is their degree of control [for weeding out other influencing factors].[25]

In addition to the elevated risk of psychiatric disorders, many gay relationships are plagued by domestic violence. Recent research reported in the *American Journal of Public Health* found that one of five gay men reported being beaten by a sex partner, and 5 percent acknowledged being raped.[26] A study of lesbian relationships, reported in the *Journal of Interpersonal Violence,* found that during a one-year period, 90 percent of the lesbians surveyed had been the victim of one or more acts of verbal aggression by their partners, while 31 percent reported one or more incidents of physical abuse.[27] The National Violence Against Women Survey, sponsored by the National Institute of Justice, found that "same-sex cohabitants reported significantly more intimate partner violence than did opposite-sex cohabitants."[28]

Certainly not all gays and lesbians struggle with mental illness, drug and alcohol addiction, or domestic violence in their relationships. However, the research clearly indicates that homosexuals are at substantially higher risk

---

[25]J. M. Bailey, "Commentary: Homosexuality and Mental Illness," *Archive of General Psychiatry* 56 (1999): 876-80.

[26]Greenwood, "Battering Victimization," pp. 1964-69.

[27]Lettie L. Lockhart et al., "Letting Out the Secret: Violence in Lesbian Relationships," *Journal of Interpersonal Violence* 9 (1994): 469-92.

[28]"Extent, Nature, and Consequences of Intimate Partner Violence," *U.S. Department of Justice: Office of Justice Programs,* July 2000, p. 30.

for many of these problems, and this should concern everyone who cares about human well-being. Unfortunately, many gays and lesbians aren't aware of how others struggle with and suffer from these issues. That's because America's gay organizations appear to have a vested interest in convincing the public that homosexuality is just as healthy as heterosexuality. High levels of psychiatric disorders, suicide and domestic violence don't make for good press when you are pressing for social normalization.

In addition to pressuring the APA to change their position on homosexuality, gay lobbying groups are entrenched within the American Psychological Association, the American Counseling Association, the National Association of Social Workers and the American Academy of Pediatrics. For example, the American Psychological Association's "Office on Lesbian, Gay, and Bisexual Concerns" approves all position statements on homosexuality made by that organization. Ignoring the research studies we have just mentioned, their website states:

> Over 35 years of objective, well-designed scientific research has shown that homosexuality, in and of itself, is not associated with mental disorders or emotional or social problems. Homosexuality was once thought to be a mental illness because mental health professionals and society had biased information.[29]

How tragic that the very professional organizations that Americans count on for accurate, objective information have been co-opted by gay lobbyists intent on advancing their own agenda. Sadly, the main victims of these misinformation campaigns are millions of gay men and lesbian women, not to mention countless numbers of young teens who are struggling with sexual-identity confusion. And this misinformation hurts people.

Many of these same organizations are directly involved in perpetrating a third myth about homosexuality, namely, that it is a fixed, unchangeable, lifetime condition.

---

[29]"Answers to Your Questions About Sexual Orientation and Homosexuality," *APA Online* <www.apa.org/pubinfo/answers.html#mentalillness>.

A WORD OF INTENT

As we conclude this chapter, it is important to make a very clear point. We do not object to homosexuality because it is "yucky" and "not how most people live." Rather, we believe that homosexual behavior should not be celebrated or encouraged because it does not serve human well-being. As Christians, we believe *every* person, including homosexual persons, has inestimable worth and value as God's image bearers. *And because people matter, their actions matter.* As a society we should seek to encourage behaviors and actions that increase health, happiness and growth for every human being so that every human being can live a healthy, happy and fulfilling life. Every Christian is compelled to love their neighbor. Tangibly caring for others' well-being demonstrates our love for them. And sometimes caring for others means being honest with them about behavior that may cause them suffering and harm.

CONCLUSION

Recent research appears to show a high prevalence of physical or psychological problems among homosexuals. Gay men are at elevated risk for a variety of sexually transmitted diseases (including HIV-AIDS), and on average they can expect a shortened life expectancy. Both gay men and lesbian women suffer from higher levels of psychiatric illness, drug and alcohol abuse, and suicide. Teenagers who experiment with homosexual behavior tend to engage in other high-risk behaviors. Domestic violence also plagues many gay relationships.

Bowing to pressure from gay activists (often within their own ranks) the major U.S. mental health organizations fail to mention these findings in their official positions on homosexuality. These groups take the position that the problems experienced by homosexuals are due to the discrimination and rejection they experience in our "homophobic society." However, many of the recent studies linking homosexuality and mental illness have been conducted in gay-affirming societies such as the Netherlands, which appears to discredit this theory.

14

CAN HOMOSEXUALS
CHANGE THEIR SEXUAL ORIENTATION?

Our friend Mike is a former homosexual. Gay activists will tell you that people like Mike don't exist. They've even shouted "You don't exist!" in his face. But Mike does exist. We've been to his house, celebrated birthdays with him and discussed the exploits of Spider-Man with his four-year-old son. Mike has been married to a charming woman for nine years, has two adorable little boys and is one of the best dads we know. We have met many of his dear friends, male and female, who have similar stories of leaving homosexuality.

Mike is the first to admit that change hasn't been easy and that many who have tried to leave homosexuality have failed. But many gay organizations claim that change is impossible and that no gay person has ever changed his or her sexual orientation. They argue that therapies designed to help homosexuals who desire change are cruel, misleading and harmful. (We believe it's cruel and misleading when these organizations tell gays who want to change that they are "foolish.") Wayne Besen, formerly of the Human Rights Campaign, denounces any therapist or organization that would dare to promote the idea that change is possible:

> They take people with extremely low self-esteem and make them feel even worse about themselves. . . . The amount of conflict, turmoil, suffering and human misery these groups cause people is astounding. . . . [Q]uite simply, ex-gays don't exist.[1]

Besen isn't alone. Gay pressure groups within several mental health organizations have succeeded in passing resolutions questioning or condemning

---

[1]"Wayne Besen: Exposing Scandals Behind the Ex-Gay Myth," an interview by Raj Ayyar, *Gay Today* 8, no. 87, March 27, 2004, <http://gaytoday.com/interview/080103in.asp>.

reorientation or "reparative" therapy (therapies that assist homosexuals who desire to change their sexual orientation). For example, the National Association of Social Workers (NASW), in its *Policy Statement on Lesbian, Gay and Bisexual Issues*, states:

> Social stigmatization of lesbian, gay, and bisexual people is widespread and is a primary motivating factor in leading some people to seek sexual orientation changes. . . . No data demonstrate that reparative or conversion therapies are effective, and in fact they may be harmful. . . . NASW discourages social workers from providing treatments designed to change sexual orientation or from referring practitioners or programs that claim to do so.[2]

QUESTION 1. *But is this statement accurate? Is it true that these therapies "may be harmful" and that there is "no data" demonstrating their effectiveness?*

ANSWER. The NASW's position is based more on *politics* than facts. Numerous research studies have been conducted on homosexuality and change. Several studies have found that in many cases homosexuals can actually change their orientation or at least eliminate unwanted homosexual behavior and fantasies.[3] The research also indicates that change can be difficult and that not all homosexuals who have attempted to change their orientation have been successful.[4] Homosexual orientation is a deeply rooted, pervasive condition that may be resistant to treatment in some cases.

Researchers who investigate the results of reorientation therapy face several challenges. First, research on therapeutic change often depends on the "self-report" of individuals who have engaged in therapy or the "therapist reports" of the professionals who conduct the therapy. This is true whether we are discussing treatment for homosexuality, depression or alcoholism. As

---

[2]"Lesbian, Gay and Bisexual Issues," *Social Work Speaks*, January 1, 2003, p. 230 <www .socialworkers.org/da/da2005/documents/lesbgaybisex.pdf>.

[3]For a thorough review, see Stanton L. Jones and Mark A. Yarhouse, *Homosexuality: The Use of Scientific Research in the Church's Moral Debate* (Downers Grove, Ill.: InterVarsity Press, 2000), pp. 117-51.

[4]Ibid.

such, the outcome literature is based on subjective experience and is subject to personal bias. Some of the research in this field has relied on rather nebulous "categories of improvement," such as "very improved," "somewhat improved" and so forth. Recent research has attempted to correct this problem by using more objective descriptions such as "exclusively heterosexual," "exclusively homosexual" or the highly technical "definite same-sex response, but strong and predominant reaction to the opposite sex." These more precise descriptions allow for more accurate measures of the degree of change.[5]

Psychiatrists and psychologists who conduct research on homosexuality and change have also found it exceedingly difficult to publish their findings. Since the major mental health organizations have adopted a "gay is OK" stance, we are unlikely to find studies on sexual-orientation change in the professional journals that they control. Funding for such research is also difficult to obtain because few universities support the notion that homosexuality is a condition that can or should be treated. In spite of these limitations, such studies do exist, and the research on reorientation therapy indicates that a substantial percentage of individuals who seek treatment for unwanted homosexuality have had successful outcomes.[6]

The most significant recent study on change was conducted by Dr. Robert Spitzer of Columbia University. Dr. Spitzer is one of the psychiatrists who led the 1973 effort to have the American Psychiatric Association remove homosexuality from the list of mental disorders. But in recent years Spitzer has become convinced that homosexuals can change their sexual orientation and remain heterosexual.

In an article published recently in the *Archives of Sexual Behavior,* Spitzer reported the results of his study of two hundred men and women who had participated in "reorientation counseling." Each of these individuals had reported "at least some minimal change" from homosexuality to heterosexuality that lasted at least five years. Spitzer found that 66 percent of the men

---

[5]Ibid.
[6]For an excellent review of this research, see W. Throckmorton, "Initial Empirical and Clinical Findings Concerning the Change Process for Ex-Gays," *Professional Psychology: Research and Practice* 33 (2002): 242-48.

and 44 percent of the women had achieved what he termed "good heterosexual functioning." In addition, 89 percent of the men and 95 percent of the women said they were bothered only "slightly" or "not at all" by unwanted homosexual feelings after such counseling.[7]

Spitzer did find that some of his subjects were still struggling with change. Of the 158 individuals who were no longer in therapy, 13 percent of the men and 10 percent of the women reported that they had experienced a brief occurrence (usually only a few days) of "overt homosexual behavior." Only 11 percent of the men and 37 percent of the women said that they had experienced a "complete" break from homosexuality—in other words, they no longer had even occasional homosexual fantasies.[8]

QUESTION 2. *So people who say such therapy is harmful are wrong?*

ANSWER. Yes, quite wrong. As mentioned earlier, gay activist organizations claim that reorientation therapy is harmful to homosexuals. They warn it offers "false hope" and leads to depression and suicide. But Dr. Spitzer's study showed just the opposite. Those who had undergone therapy experienced much less depression. Forty-three percent of the men and 47 percent of the women reported being "markedly" or "extremely" depressed *before* therapy. *After* therapy, only 1 percent of the men and 4 percent of the women reported having been depressed at any time during the year prior to the study.[9] According to Spitzer,

> Participants reported benefit from nonsexual changes, such as decreased depression, a greater sense of masculinity in males, and femininity in females, and developing intimate nonsexual relations with members of the same sex.[10]

Spitzer's critics dispute his findings, claiming that because many of the study's subjects were referred by Christian "ex-gay" ministries, they either

---

[7]R. L. Spitzer, "Can Some Gay Men and Lesbians Change Their Sexual Orientation? 200 Participants Reporting a Change from Homosexual to Heterosexual Orientation," *Archives of Sexual Behavior* 32, no. 5 (2003): 403-17.
[8]Ibid., p. 410.
[9]Ibid., p. 412.
[10]Ibid., p. 413.

had an "agenda," exaggerated the truth or weren't really homosexual to begin with but were "bisexual." For example, John Bancroft, a professor at In-
diana University, argues, "Given their powerful agenda of promoting such
treatment, it would be surprising if they did not overestimate the amount
of change."[11] Spitzer counters that if the subjects were lying, they wouldn't
have admitted that they continued to struggle with some measure of homosexual feelings: "If there was significant bias, one might expect that many
participants would report complete or near complete change in all sexual
orientation measures."[12] But the individuals who participated in the study
were willing to admit that in some cases they still struggled with homosexual attraction.

It should be noted that Spitzer's research didn't include a representative,
"random sampling" of all homosexuals. Since he only interviewed individuals who said they had successfully changed, his study can't tell us the overall
percentage of gays and lesbians who might experience a positive outcome in
reorientation therapy. But his study doesn't *attempt* to answer that question.
It simply attempts to determine whether successful change *is possible*. He
found that it was clearly possible.

Why do gay organizations have such a vested interest in convincing the
general public that reorientation therapy is ineffective and that ex-gays don't
exist? Columnist Ethan Campbell points out that if therapy *does* work and
homosexuals *can* change, the gay lobby has a lot to lose:

> To understand the purpose behind such weak-minded attacks, we
> must look at what is at stake politically for the attackers. In most
> states, gay and lesbian groups are fighting to gain "equal rights," a term
> that means anything from hiring quotas to legal marriages to state-
> funded sex changes. In order to win certain types of equal rights, the
> gay lobby must prove that sexual orientation is as unchanging as, say,
> race or gender. Any evidence to the contrary, any hint that it might be

---

[11]John Bancroft, "Can Sexual Orientation Change? A Long-Running Saga," part of "Peer Com-
mentaries on Spitzer (2003)," *Archives of Sexual Behavior* 32, no. 5 (2003): 420.
[12]Ibid., p. 412.

fluid or at all a matter of choice, undercuts these political goals.[13]

The truth is that many homosexuals have found hope and healing through reorientation therapy. Change does not happen overnight. And for many, establishing a new sexual identity is a lifelong journey, with many bumps and potholes along the road. But the claim that no homosexual has ever truly changed his or her sexual orientation to heterosexual is simply false and motivated by a political agenda. It is not motivated by human concern.

Ruben Fine, the former director of the New York Center for Psychoanalytic Training, has stated that the "misinformation spread by certain circles that homosexuality is untreatable" has done "incalculable harm to thousands."[14] In the 1970s, sex researchers Masters and Johnson wrote that the view that "homosexuality cannot be changed [is] certainly open to question."[15] And based on the research data, Dr. Stanton Jones, the provost and former chair of the psychology department at Wheaton College, warns: "Anyone who says there is no hope [for change] is either ignorant or a liar."[16]

Perhaps no one counters gay activist claims about "normalcy" and "the harmful effects of therapy" better than lesbian author Camille Paglia. In her book *Vamps and Tramps,* Paglia argues, "Gay activists are guilty of Stalinist disinformation when they assert that homosexuality is no different than and equivalent to heterosexuality. . . . Is gay identity so fragile that it cannot bear the thought that some people may not wish to be gay?"[17]

The real tragedy of such disinformation is that millions of gays and lesbians (many of whom are unhappy with their orientation and deeply desire change) are being told by the media, professional mental health organizations and people who supposedly are their *advocates* that change is impossible and that attempting to change will only lead to frustration, hopelessness

---

[13]Ethan Campbell, "Score One for Politics," *Boundless,* <www.boundless.org/2000/features/a0000445.html>.

[14]Ruben Fine, "Psychoanalytic Theory," in *Male and Female Homosexuality: Psychological Approaches,* ed. Louis Diamant (New York: Hemisphere, 1987), pp. 84-86.

[15]William H. Masters and Virginia E. Johnson, *Homosexuality in Perspective* (Boston: Little, Brown, 1979), p. 402.

[16]Stanton Jones, "The Loving Opposition," *Christianity Today,* July 19, 1993, p. 25.

[17]Camille Paglia, *Vamps and Tramps* (New York: Vintage Books, 1994), pp. 71, 77.

and depression. Even worse, thousands of distressed, struggling teenagers are completely unaware that treatment is available for their sexual identity confusion. In light of the devastating consequences of homosexual behavior, such duplicity seems selfish, callous and cruel.

The myths that homosexuality is inborn, normal and unchangeable are promulgated by gay organizations to advance their political goals—including their goal of obtaining nationwide same-sex marriage—at the expense of people seeking wholeness and happiness in life. These myths crumble under the scrutiny of science.

CONCLUSION

The psychological research indicates that many homosexuals who have desired to change their sexual orientation have been successful in doing so. Change can be difficult, and some former homosexuals continue to struggle with residual feelings of same-sex attraction. But thousands of men and women have successfully left homosexuality and report happy, fulfilling lives. Gay organizations deny that real change is possible, for if it were, it would mean that sexual orientation can be modified, severely hampering their efforts to equate homosexuality with race or ethnicity. For this reason they engage in intensive lobbying within the professional mental health organizations, urging them to condemn or prohibit therapies that may lead to the successful "reorientation" that many have desired and successfully obtained. Question: Is it compassionate to prevent (or attempt to scare) individuals who are unhappy with their sexual orientation from receiving treatment that may offer them real hope? We believe such actions are rooted in an effort to tie people to special-interest politics and are a blatant attempt to limit human freedom. So do our ex-gay friends.

15

Do All Homosexuals
Want to Get Married?

Listening to gay activists argue for same-sex marriage on the cable TV talk shows, you might get the impression that homosexuals are of one mind on this issue. But the reality is that the gay community is seriously divided over the prospect of same-sex marriage.

While some homosexual couples desire a life similar to married heterosexuals—quiet, domestic life in the suburbs—others view marriage as a ball and chain that would constrain a more socially radical "queer identity" of no-boundaries hedonism and promiscuity.[1] Still others (mainly lesbian "family law" scholars) argue for the complete deconstruction of marriage, which they view as "archaic," "patriarchal" and "oppressive."[2] These individuals seek to dismantle the structures of traditional marriage, arguing instead for no definitive family categories.[3] But Dr. Paul Nathanson represents another mindset of homosexuals. He contends it is risky to tinker with the institution of marriage and that legalizing same-sex unions could endanger the health and well-being of our society.[4]

---

[1]On the one hand, see Andrew Sullivan, "Here Comes the Groom: A Conservative Case for Gay Marriage," *The New Republic*, August 28, 1989; and on the other see Jim Rinnert, "The Trouble with Gay Marriage," *In These Times*, December 30, 2003; Judith Levine, "Stop the Wedding! Why Gay Marriage Isn't Radical Enough," *The Village Voice*, July 23-29, 2003 <www.villagevoice.com /issues/0330/levine.php>.

[2]Paula Ettelbrick, "Since When Is Marriage a Path to Liberation?" *OUT/LOOK National Gay and Lesbian Quarterly* 6 (1989); Nancy Polikoff, "An End to All Marriage," *The Washington Blade*, July 25, 2003.

[3]See Stanley Kurtz, "Beyond Gay Marriage," *The Weekly Standard*, August 4-11, 2003.

[4]See Paul Nathanson and Katherine Young, "Marriage a la Mode: Answering Advocates of Gay Marriage," p. 2 (paper presented at Emory University in Atlanta, Ga., May 14, 2003). A copy of the paper can be accessed at <www.family.org.au/journal/2003/j20030703.html>.

QUESTION 1. *Why is it important to become familiar with these different positions?*

ANSWER. As you examine the arguments for and against same-sex marriage, it's important to realize that the homosexual community is not monolithic. Not all homosexuals are clamoring for marriage. There are many different views about marriage within the gay community. An overview of the four major positions follows in this answer and the answers to the next three questions.

The first group is those making what they call "the conservative case for same-sex marriage." Some of the most articulate and reasoned voices in this crowd are journalists Andrew Sullivan and Jonathan Rauch and attorney Evan Wolfson. These three write and speak extensively about same-sex marriage to both gays and straights, arguing that homosexual couples are capable of attaining the same level of relational health and commitment enjoyed by happily married heterosexual couples. All are opposed to civil unions or domestic partnerships, which they view as a two-tiered "separate but equal" system.[5] They contend that homosexual couples are entitled to every right and benefit bestowed on married heterosexuals, and they challenge their peers in the gay community to aspire to responsible marriages characterized by monogamy and fidelity (although Rauch is more sober in his view of whether this would be possible).[6]

In his essay "All Together Now," Wolfson writes about some of the committed gay couples he knows. He encourages other homosexuals to publicly share their own stories of relational success.

> Let's also convey the strengths and vibrancy of many gay and lesbian couples such as my former clients Richard and Ron, who just celebrated their 31st anniversary, or my friends Jamie and Mark, who gathered friends and family from around the country to celebrate their wedding in a lovely church ceremony. Let's make sure that America

---

[5]Jonathan Rauch, *Gay Marriage: Why Its Good for Gays, Good for Straights, and Good for America* (New York: Henry Holt, 2004); Evan Wolfson, "All Together Now," in *Marriage and Same-Sex Unions: A Debate,* ed. Lynn Wardle et al. (Westport, Conn.: Praeger, 2003); Andrew Sullivan, "Marriage or Bust: Why Civil Unions Aren't Enough," *The New Republic,* April 27, 2000 <www.andrewsullivan.com/homosexuality.php?artnum=20000427>.
[6]Rauch, *Gay Marriage,* pp. 145-46.

hears the voice of Jamie's father, describing his growth in acceptance and wish that society could now do the same.[7]

While these three make impassioned pleas for the legal benefits of marriage, it seems clear that what is most important to them is society's recognition and affirmation of gay relationships. For that reason they argue that civil unions are an unacceptable alternative. Sullivan compares them to the "miscegenation" laws that once prohibited interracial marriage in our country.

If civil union gives homosexuals everything marriage grants heterosexuals, why the fuss? First, because such an arrangement once again legally divides Americans with regard to our central social institution. Like the miscegenation laws, civil union essentially creates a two-tiered system, with one marriage model clearly superior to the other. The benefits may be the same, as they were for black couples, but the segregation is just as profound. . . . [Marriage] affirms a civil equality that emanates outward to the rest of our society. To carve within it a new, segregated partition is to make the same mistake we made with miscegenation.[8]

One of the more interesting arguments advanced by these authors is that same-sex marriage will domesticate gay men. Although the latest social-science research doesn't support this notion (see chapter two), Sullivan is hopeful:

The truth is that there is little evidence that same-sex marriages will be less successful than straight marriages. Because marriage will be a new experience for most gay people, one they have struggled for decades to achieve, its privileges will not be taken for granted. My own bet is that gay marriages may well turn out to be more responsible, serious, and committed than straight ones.[9]

For Rauch, Wolfson and Sullivan, same-sex marriage will provide gay couples new rights and privileges, moral legitimacy, and the incentive to forsake promiscuity and "settle down with that special someone." As gay intel-

---

[7]Wolfson, "All Together Now," p. 8.
[8]Sullivan, "Marriage or Bust."
[9]Ibid.

lectuals they regularly make that case on university campuses, television news programs and in the print media. But their position is at odds with others in the gay community.

QUESTION 2. *What is different about the marriage beliefs of others in the gay community?*

ANSWER. A second group of homosexuals has no interest in marriage. For these gays and lesbians the thought of participating in a traditional marriage ceremony doesn't bring joy to their hearts. Instead, it provokes anxiety and even revulsion. These individuals view marriage as conformist, confining and diametrically opposed to everything that "gay liberation" represents. They are all for equal rights and benefits, but they believe that affirming marriage—gay or straight—works against this.

Jim Rinnert, of *In These Times* magazine, articulates this view in an editorial titled "The Trouble with Gay Marriage." Rinnert states that when he is asked for his thoughts about same-sex marriage, he answers "I'm against it."

> Gay marriage strikes me as, first and foremost, just another way to show the straights we're the same as them, that we're as "normal" as the heterosexuals with whom we share the planet and thereby are worthy of acceptance into their club. . . . [G]uess what—we're not the same. We're different. Rather than try to paint heterosexual stripes on our pelts, let's examine, explore, and celebrate our different coloration.[10]

Rinnert contends that there is a divide within the gay community, with the "leather boys, drag queens, and bare-chested dykes" at one end of the "parade" and the "political seekers and Dignity members" (the first group we examined) at the other. He reminds his readers that marriage is a "heterosexual institution. . . . [A] term with a specific meaning and history," and he argues that the gay community has no business getting tangled up in it.

Let them have it—the term and the institution. To engage in that

---

[10]Jim Rinnert, "The Trouble with Gay Marriage," *In These Times*, December 30, 2003 <www.inthesetimes.com/site/main/article/the_trouble_with_gay_marriage>.

argument is to be sidetracked by semantics. . . . If you want to register at Target and get lots of stuff when you "wed," do it. Let heterosexual men and women have their institution and their name for it; we need to find the imagination and the guts to visualize and build our own.[11]

This camp sees homosexual culture and the heterosexual-marriage culture as drastic opposites. If same-sex marriage becomes legal in our country, Camille Paglia doubts that we will see a profound change in the nature of male gay relationships:

My experience is that gay men's idea of marriage or any kind of relationship is rather open. That's why a lot of people are a little skeptical. Gay men—they're "together for 30 years": what does that mean? That means they go out and pick up strangers every two weeks.[12]

After the Canadian province of Ontario legalized same-sex marriage in 2003, the *New York Times* ran an informative article by Clifford Krauss titled "Free to Marry, Canada's Gays Say, 'Do I'?" It documented the fact that few Canadian gay couples rushed to the altar after the historic ruling. In fact, many of the couples Krauss interviewed expressed reservations about the very concept of marriage.

When David Andrew, a forty-one-year-old federal government employee, heard that the highest Ontario court had extended marriage rights to same-sex couples . . . he broke into a sweat. "I was dreading the conversation," he said, fearing that his partner would feel jilted when he told him that he did not believe in the institution. "Personally, I saw marriage as a dumbing down of gay relationships. My dread is that soon you will have a complacent bloc of gay and lesbian soccer moms."[13]

---

[11]Ibid.

[12]Camille Paglia, "Connubial Personae," in *Same Sex Marriage: Pro and Con*, ed. Andrew Sullivan (New York: Vintage Books, 1997), p. 140.

[13]Clifford Krauss, "Free to Marry, Canada's Gays Say, 'Do I'?" *New York Times*, August 31, 2003, sec. 1, p. 1.

Mr. Andrew and his partner of seven years told Krauss that they "stop short of monogamy in their committed relationship, which is something [they] do not believe in."[14]

Krauss also discussed the Ontario ruling with Mitchel Raphael, editor and chief of *Fab*, a popular gay magazine in Toronto. Raphael confirmed that few Canadian homosexuals were embracing same-sex marriage.

Ambiguity is a good word for the feeling among gays about marriage. I'd be for marriage if I thought gay people would challenge and change the institution and not buy into the traditional meaning of "till death do us part" and monogamy forever. We should be Oscar Wildes and not like everyone else watching the play.[15]

The *Times* article included a revealing quote from Rinaldo Walcott, a gay sociologist at the University of Toronto, who warned that same-sex marriage could be "an agent of homogenization."

I can already hear folks saying things like: "Why are the bathhouses needed? Straights don't have them." Will queers now have to live with the heterosexual forms of guilt with something called cheating?[16]

The resistance to same-sex marriage expressed by columnist Rinnert and those interviewed for the *New York Times* may indicate that some homosexuals, particularly gay men, are simply not "the marrying kind." Social science research would seem to support that view. A 2004 report from the University of Chicago indicated that 61 percent of the men in Chicago's gay community had more than thirty sexual partners, with 43 percent of that group reporting more than sixty partners.[17]

This camp opposes same-sex marriage primarily because they believe it would squelch the sexual liberty that, for them, is a primary virtue of being gay.

---

[14]Ibid.
[15]Ibid.
[16]Ibid.
[17]Adrian Brune, "City Gays Skip Long-term Relationships: Study Says," *Washington Blade*, February 27, 2004, p. 12.

QUESTION 3. *What about the third group of gays you mentioned?*

ANSWER. While the first group is seen as more conservative, seeking committed domesticity, and the second group is more apathetic toward marriage, the third group is downright revolutionary. They want to upset everyone's thinking on marriage and family. Paula Ettelbrick has spoken a long time for this group. She said in the late eighties:

> We must keep our eyes on the goals of providing true alternatives to marriage and of *radically reordering society's view of family.* . . . We must not fool ourselves into believing that marriage will make it acceptable to be gay or lesbian.[18]

This group of gays seeks to *deconstruct* the institution of marriage itself. These individuals view traditional marriage as an elitist, oppressive, patriarchal institution that must be dismantled for the sake of individual freedom and the evolution of society. They believe that once same-sex marriage becomes commonplace and accepted by the masses, it is only a short step to legalized polygamy, polyamory (group marriage) and the abandonment of all gender and familial norms.[19]

The leading figures in this marriage "deconstructionist" movement are family law scholars at leading institutions. This group includes Ettelbrick, who teaches law at New York University and Columbia University; Nancy Polikoff, a law professor at American University; Martha Fineman at Cornell University; Martha Ertman at the University of Utah; Judith Stacey at New York University, a sociologist rather than a professor of law; David Chambers at the University of Michigan; and Martha Minow of Harvard Law School. [20]

Ettelbrick's writings on same-sex marriage are representative of the gay deconstructionists:

> Being queer is more than setting up house, sleeping with a person of

---

[18]Ettelbrick, "Since When Is Marriage a Path to Liberation?" p. 120 (emphasis added).
[19]Stanley Kurtz, "Beyond Gay Marriage," *Weekly Standard*, August 4-11, 2003, pp. 26-33.
[20]Ibid., p. 29.

the same gender, and seeking state approval for doing so. . . . Being queer means pushing the parameters of sex, sexuality and family, and in the process transforming the very fabric of society.[21]

In her essay "Since When Is Marriage a Path to Liberation?" Ettelbrick cautions gays and lesbians about pursuing same-sex marriage in order to "make us feel good about ourselves":

> Marriage will not liberate us as lesbians and gay men. In fact, it will constrain us, make us more invisible, force our assimilation into the mainstream, and undermine the goals of gay liberation. . . . Marriage runs contrary to two of the primary goals of the lesbian and gay movement: the affirmation of gay identity and culture and the validation of many forms of relationships.[22]

American University's Polikoff echoed Ettelbrick's admonition to the gay community in an opinion piece that appeared in the *Washington Blade* shortly after the U.S. Supreme Court's *Lawrence v. Texas* decision.

> The majesty of the Supreme Court's rhetoric should push the gay and lesbian movement in another direction: abolishing the legal status of marriage for everyone. . . . Gay marriage will move us in the wrong direction if it limits legal recognition to married couples only.[23]

Publicly, both Ettelbrick and Polikoff support same-sex marriage, and they are frequently quoted by the press. Why? According to Stanley Kurtz at the Hoover Institution, they and the other family law radicals hope to use gay marriage to pave the way for the legalization of group marriage and the concomitant demise of all family categories. Kurtz cites an article in the *Michigan Law Review* in which the University of Michigan's David Chambers encourages those who oppose traditional marriage to *support* same-sex unions in order to make society more accepting of further legal changes.

[21]Ettelbrick, "Since When Is Marriage a Path to Liberation?" cited in *Same Sex Marriage: Pro and Con,* ed. Andrew Sullivan (New York: Vintage Books: 1997), p. 120.

[22]Ibid., pp. 119-20.

[23]Nancy Polikoff, "An End to All Marriage," *Washington Blade,* July 25, 2003, <http://washblade.com/2003/7-25/view/columns/endmarriage.cfm>.

By ceasing to conceive of marriage as a partnership composed of one person of each sex, the state may become more receptive to units of three or more. . . . All desirable changes in family law need not be made at once.[24]

Are Ettelbrick, Polikoff, Chambers and the other advocates of polyamory simply a bunch of nutty academics?[25] No. Their push to make all close, personal relationships socially equal is gaining some very influential supporters. Both the American Law Institute's recent *Principles of the Law of Family Dissolution* as well as the Law Commission of Canada's 2001 report *Beyond Conjugality: Recognizing and Supporting Close Personal Relationships* advocate elevating all close, personal relationships to the legal status of marriage, and as a result eliminating marriage as a legal and domestic category.[26]

Kurtz is convinced that if same-sex marriage is legalized in our country, polyamory won't be far behind, which will mean there will no longer be the legal category of "family." Given the "hostility of the legal elite to traditional marriage," he argues that the only sure-fire way to protect it is through something like the Federal Marriage Amendment to the U.S. Constitution. Without such protection, Kurtz fears what the future may hold:

Marriage is a critical social institution. Stable families depend on it. Society depends on stable families. Up to now, with all the changes in marriage, the one thing we've been sure of is that marriage means monogamy. Gay marriage will break that connection. . . . What lies beyond gay marriage is no marriage at all.[27]

QUESTION 4. *Are there any gay voices that support natural marriage?*

ANSWER. There are, and they show that being for natural marriage and against same-sex marriage isn't rooted in homophobia. Some homosexuals

---

[24]Kurtz, "Beyond Gay Marriage," p. 29.

[25]For a definition of *polyamory* see the answer to question five of chapter one (p. 27).

[26]See *Principles of the Law of Family Dissolution,* published by the American Law Institute in 2002; and *Beyond Conjugality: Recognizing and Supporting Close Personal Adult Relationships,* published by the Law Commission of Canada, Ottawa, in 2001.

[27]Kurtz, "Beyond Gay Marriage," p. 33.

believe marriage should not be redefined, because marriage is too important to tamper with. Although the majority of gay individuals probably fall into one of the three camps mentioned earlier in this chapter, there are a few who have publicly stated that same-sex marriage might negatively affect men, women, children and society. Perhaps the most articulate spokesperson for this position is Paul Nathanson, a researcher in religious studies at McGill University in Toronto, Canada. Professor Nathanson and his colleague Katherine Young (who is heterosexual) have written a powerful point-by-point rebuttal to the most common same-sex marriage arguments. Their paper "Marriage a la Mode: Answering Advocates of Gay Marriage" was first presented at a family conference at Emory University in 2003.[28]

Nathanson and Young don't believe there is anything inherently wrong with gay relationships. But they contend that same-sex marriage will harm society because "marriage between men and women—must be publicly fostered by culture and supported by law."

Nathanson and Young contend that the advocates of same-sex marriage ignore all of the societal loads natural marriage must carry (that we have explored in this book). That's because, for the most part, gay activists are radical individualists who show little concern for the greater culture.

> This indifference to society as a whole is made clear by those who defend gay marriage. Allowing gay people to marry, they say, would be beneficial to gay individuals (or to the gay community). How could that, they ask, harm straight individuals (or the straight community)? But advocates of gay marriage have made no serious attempt to consider the possible harms and object to those who want more time to assess the evidence from other periods or other cultures.[29]

As mentioned in chapter eleven, one of the main reasons that same-sex marriage is even *thinkable* today is that heterosexuals have already redefined marriage to suit their own individualistic tastes. Nathanson and Young examine the current marriage milieu and warn what may lie ahead if same-sex

---

[28]Nathanson and Young, "Marriage a la Mode."
[29]Ibid.

marriage becomes the law of the land.

> Over and over again, advocates of gay marriage say precisely what straight people have been saying about marriage for decades: that it is strictly about public recognition for the love between two individuals. . . . Children have very little to do with marriage (except for those who either have produced or will produce children in order to satisfy their personal desires as individual adults).[30]

Drs. Nathanson and Young make a compelling case that legalizing same-sex marriage will ultimately harm all of us. And since Nathanson is gay, it's difficult to claim he's motivated by intolerance or homophobia. Quite to the contrary; he simply understands the importance of natural marriage and places *the greater good of society* above his own personal preferences. Unfortunately, this concept seems lost on those advocating the redefinition of marriage. As professors Nathanson and Young warn: "We cannot predict the future of this experiment. As we say, people are not like rats in a lab. Mistakes are much more costly."[31]

CONCLUSION

The gay community doesn't speak with one voice about same-sex marriage. In fact, homosexual individuals have widely varying opinions as to the merits of entering into a marital relationship. A few gay spokespersons call for redefining the institution of marriage to include gay and lesbian couples. They argue this will be good for society and cause gay men to "settle down." Another group of homosexuals want nothing to do with marriage, viewing it as a restrictive ball and chain, completely incompatible with the so-called sexual freedom of the gay culture. A third group, represented by a few elite family law scholars at some of the nation's leading universities, advocates for deconstructing marriage altogether. They argue that the government should sanction all relationships of any conceivable make up and size, regardless of gender, sexual orientation, number of partners or age. Finally, other homo-

---

[30]Ibid.
[31]Ibid.

sexuals warn that redefining marriage will have profound negative consequences for society. When discussing the same-sex marriage issue with friends and family, it's helpful to understand the wide diversity of opinion within the gay community on this issue.

Cheat Sheet for Section III

Myth 1. Homosexuals Are "Born Gay"
Several studies in the early 1990s appeared to indicate that homosexuality might have a biological basis.

1. Each of those studies suffered from serious methodological flaws, and their results have not been duplicated. The gay researchers who conducted these studies have stated publicly that their research did not prove that homosexuality is inborn.

2. Other research recognizes possible familial or psychological causes for homosexuality (such as family dysfunction or early sexual abuse).

3. The current consensus in the scientific community is that homosexuality is likely caused by the complex interaction of biological, psychological and social factors.

Myth 2. Homosexuality Is "Normal and Natural"
As a group, homosexuals have a much higher incidence of significant health and psychological problems than do heterosexuals.

1. In 1973, the American Psychiatric Association declassified homosexuality as a mental disorder. This decision was not based on new research but on immense political pressure from gay activists.

2. Teenagers who experiment with homosexual behavior tend to engage in other high-risk behaviors.

3. Recent research conducted in the Netherlands (a very gay-friendly country where same-sex marriage is legal) found that both gay men and lesbian women have a much higher incidence of psychiatric disorders, drug and alcohol abuse, suicide, and higher incidences of infidelity.

4. Domestic violence is more common in the gay community than among heterosexuals. One out of five gay men report being beaten by a sex partner; 5 percent acknowledge being raped by a partner.

5. Most professional mental health organizations either fail to acknowledge the negative research on homosexuality or attribute the problems to "homophobia." Gay activists are influential within these organizations and typically craft the organizations' professional positions on homosexuality.

Myth 3. Homosexuals Can't Change Their Sexual Orientation

Many homosexuals who have desired to change their sexual orientation have been successful.

1. Gay organizations have a vested political interest in denying that change is possible, so they have pressured the major mental health organizations to prohibit or discourage therapies that may help homosexuals to successfully change.

2. Researchers who investigate the effectiveness of reorientation therapies face both methodological and political challenges. Even so, numerous scientific studies validate that while change may be difficult, it is definitely possible.

3. Dr. Robert Spitzer of Columbia University conducted one of the most recent large-scale studies on the possibility of change. He found that individuals who were highly motivated (often by religious beliefs) were able to change their orientation from homosexual to heterosexual.

4. Gay activist organizations have disputed Spitzer's research and claim that reorientation therapies offer "false hope" and will only lead to failure and depression.

Myth 4. All Homosexuals Want to Get Married

Contrary to media reports, there are widely varying opinions about same-sex marriage in the gay community.

1. Some gay leaders advocate for same-sex marriage, claiming that it will cause gay men to become monogamous and "settle down." Research data indicate this is unlikely. They also decry civil unions as "unacceptable."

2. Many homosexuals want nothing to do with marriage, saying that it would be too "restrictive" and is incompatible with gay culture.

3. Some of the nation's leading family law scholars believe that marriage should be completely deconstructed. They view marriage as a patriarchal institution and advocate for government recognition of group marriage or no marriage at all. These scholars see same-sex marriage as an efficient step toward destroying the entire institution of marriage.

4. Some homosexuals warn that redefining marriage so that gender

doesn't matter will have profound negative consequences for society. They argue that if a culture is to thrive, flourish and effectively care for its children, heterosexual marriage must be unique, supported and encouraged.

CONCLUSION:
A CHRISTIAN UNDERSTANDING OF MARRIAGE

Why does the issue of same-sex marriage matter? Why should any of us care about how marriage and the family are defined and seek to persuade those around us about this importance?

We have addressed a host of compelling reasons from the medical, psychological and social sciences on why marriage matters and why it must remain—in the ideal—a permanent, caring relationship between a man and a woman (and their common children). But all of these reasons don't stand on their own. They are supported by and find their ultimate purpose in a larger story. We will close by connecting the value of marriage with this larger story.

This larger story is the historic Christian reality, which has something unique and profound to say about the issue at hand. And while some same-sex marriage proponents say marriage is a Christian institution (in making their case that the state shouldn't support religion by supporting marriage), they are partly wrong and partly right. They are *wrong* in that if marriage were *just* a Christian institution, we would find marriage only in places where Christianity is influential as a faith system. But we find marriage in *every* culture, even those before the founding of Christianity. And they are *right* because we find marriage in all human cultures at all times for the very reason that the God of nature has wired the need for marriage into humanity.

In the beginning, God created man and placed him on a perfect, beautiful earth. Man had unfettered access and communion with God. (The Fall into sin had not yet taken place.) Everything was perfect—everything except for one thing. God declared every part of creation "good," but there was one thing that was not good. God said, "It is not good for the man to be alone" (Genesis 2:18). God was not admitting a flaw in his design but rather expressing something very important about humans.

The first chapter of Genesis tells that humans were created to show forth the image and likeness of God. We are created in the image of the triune God, who is mysteriously One but also a community of Three: one God revealed in three divine persons—Father, Son and Holy Spirit. God has existed eternally as an intimate community of loving persons. We are created in *this* image, to live with the qualities that mark the Trinity: love, intimacy and community. This is why it was not good for the man to be alone. In his aloneness, he didn't mirror the image of the triune God. So God provided the answer to the man's problem. Animals weren't the answer. Another man wasn't Adam's answer. He needed someone who shared his humanity but was also different from him. He needed someone to complete him. And God gave Adam what he needed: a woman. God blessed Adam and Eve and called them to cleave to one another and become one flesh.

Man and woman in marriage become the fullest representation of the trinitarian God on earth (Genesis 1:26-28). In this, we become what we were created to be. Psychologist and Christian theologian Mary Stewart Van Leeuwen explains in her book *Gender & Grace:*

> We cannot even develop as full persons unless we grow up in nurturing contact with others. Moreover, the fulfillment of our sociability depends on fellowship with the opposite sex. This does not mean that everyone has to marry in order to be fully human, but it does mean that subcultures of men and women only (whether this is in an enforced prison setting or a freely chosen community) are something less than human.[1]

She is exactly right. Same-sex families seeking equality with the natural family devalue humanity because they proclaim that one part of humanity is unnecessary. Women help men become what they are created to be, and men help women become what they are created to be. To deny this is to deny our full, God-given humanity. Men and women need each other, and mar-

---

[1]Mary Stewart Van Leeuwen, *Gender & Grace* (Downers Grove, Ill.: InterVarsity Press, 1990), p. 41.

riage is where we most fully and completely come together. C. S. Lewis helps us understand the depth of this truth:

> The Christian idea of marriage is based on Christ's words that a man and wife are to be regarded as a single organism—for that is what the words "one flesh" would be in modern English. And the Christians believe that when He said this He was not expressing a sentiment but stating a fact—just as one is stating a fact when one says that a lock and its key are one mechanism, or that a violin and a bow are one musical instrument. The inventor of the human machine was telling us that its two halves, the male and the female, were made to be combined together in pairs, not simply on the sexual level, but totally combined.[2]

Marriage provides good things for men and women because marriage brings men and women together into something that is larger than themselves individually. In fact, men and women coming together in marriage is larger than anything in the world, far grander than any of us realize, for it is the closest earthly reflection of the inner life of the triune God.[3] While two, they are one flesh, and this coming together as one flesh can produce the third part of this human trinity: children. It is a great mystery that only happens in heterosexuality.

The value of marriage is found in the complementary differences of male and female. "Marriages" of members of the same sex fail by definition to provide this beautiful and beneficial dynamic for both adults and children; they actually deny the very image of God in creation by denying the unity of male and female in one flesh. They say it is not necessary.

And in this very thing—by denying that husband and wives, mothers and fathers, are essential for the family—Satan accelerates his attack on God to a new level, not by challenging God's word as he did at the Fall ("Did God really say?" Genesis 3:1) but rather by challenging *God's very image* in the

---

[2]C. S. Lewis, *Mere Christianity* (New York: MacMillan, 1960), pp. 95-96.
[3]This important idea is addressed more fully in Glenn T. Stanton, *My Crazy, Imperfect Christian Family* (Colorado Springs: NavPress, 2004), chap. 3.

world (Genesis 1:26-28). All those who love God must not miss the insidiousness and depth of this attack.

The church must become equally active and passionate in two areas:

- loving and seeking the redemption of those that Satan is using and manipulating in this attack.

- protecting the triune image of God in creation by proclaiming why male and female are essential for the family and humanity.

God, give your church a measure of your grace, wisdom and favor as we commit ourselves to these two tasks.

That is our prayer.

APPENDIX
IS THERE HOPE FOR THE HOMOSEXUAL?

A Discussion on Change and Hope
with Mike Haley and Melissa Fryrear

Mike and Melissa are dear friends of ours. We work together and enjoy spending time with each other outside of work. They are great people who have similar and also very different stories. Mike and Melissa lived homosexually for many years. They came to it in different ways, and they left it in different ways. But they both now work with a ministry of Focus on the Family called *Love Won Out,* an effort to support the church and families to compassionately help those struggling with homosexuality. They have each dedicated over a decade of their lives to helping people find a way out of unwanted homosexual feelings.

We interviewed Mike and Melissa as we were finishing this book because we wanted to end with a message of hope *for* those struggling with unwanted homosexual desires. Those struggling with such desires shouldn't feel like they have to learn to continually live with such struggles. There is hope of change. Thousands of people have successfully left homosexuality and gone on to live happy, productive heterosexual lives. We know many of them. Mike and Melissa are but two, and here are their stories.

Question. Mike, can you tell us how you believe your same-sex attraction first developed?

Mike. It goes back very early. My father, because of his definition of masculinity being athleticism, pushed me quite hard and in doing so would verbally ridicule me, referring to me as "Michelle" rather than Michael and calling me his third daughter. He thought it would toughen me up, but it only hurt. And so a healthy invitation to masculinity was not present at a very young age, and I became a momma's boy. I think there I wasn't able to meet an emotional need to be accepted. That God-given homo-emotional need that we all have to fit in with our same-sex peers was never met, and so that was the genesis of it. I began to identify more with the feminine.

Question. When you began to identify more with the feminine, were you identifying with your mom or your two sisters?

Mike. Probably both. More with my sisters because I really loved them. They were ten to twelve years older than me, and they were very popular in high school—cheerleaders and homecoming queen types. I was used to being around older people, and I had a hard time bonding with my peer group because I was used to hanging out with girls and older people, who I bonded with. I never wanted to be a girl, but part of it was that the environment around me was so strongly feminine because Dad worked all the time. He owned sporting goods stores and was trying to keep food on the table. My world was feminine because when I was five, six, seven, my sisters were fifteen, sixteen, seventeen. What is a girl's dream at that age? All they ever talked about was boys, boys, boys, and so part of me has always wondered if I was also modeled to look at young boys as well because I so identified with my sisters' world.

Question. Because they were looking at boys and talking about boys?

Mike. Yes, because they were always looking at boys, making comments about them and totally intrigued about the masculine. I know that that had to have played into my confusion—wondering why everything was fixated on masculinity—and sixteen- and seventeen-year-old girls were definitely fixated on men and boys. I think some of that drew out my own mystique I had toward the masculine world, because I was definitely not comfortable there. It was "other" for me, just like it was for my sisters.

Question. When did you first sense that you were attracted to the same sex?

Mike. Very early, frankly. Before even puberty hit I realized that I had attraction there, that I had intrigue there. I was involved in childhood sex play from a very early age. It really kicked into gear at the age of eleven when that man abused me.

Question. Why don't you share that important part of your story?

Mike. It really kicked in at the age of eleven when a man who worked with my father in his sporting goods store began to pay a lot of attention to me. He kind of pulled me in, was very friendly toward me, took me surfing and invested in my life. A couple of months later the attention turned sexual. And at that stage of life a prepubescent male child is very interested in the sexual component of life. When you are introduced to these things from a very early age they hold a lot of weight, power and significance, and so he was very sexually active with me, and that played a lot into the intrigue. I think the homosexuality took root in my life during that period.

Question. You use the word *intrigue,* and we have heard other former homosexuals talk of the mystery or intrigue of the same sex. You are really not sure about who you are. You wonder what it's like to really be a boy or man. Does that resonate with you?

Mike. Yes, absolutely. If you think about how a normal child develops—I hate to use the word *normal* but you know what I mean—a child that develops in a healthy way is identified with his same-sex peer group. So let's take a young boy. He grows up and is identified in a healthy way with his same-sex peers, and when puberty kicks in for him, he is drawn to the object of difference or the object of curiosity—the "other." For a well-adjusted young boy that would be the female society. Girls are different, and he doesn't know their world; he doesn't know who they are.

But for me, and for most prehomosexual boys (as we tend to call them), they feel insecure, and the male world holds a lot of *mystique,* to use that word again. They don't feel identified, like they fit in there, but yet they know that's where they're supposed to be. And so often when puberty kicks in, that unmet emotional need or that desire to fit in is sexualized, and that's often how we see homosexuality take root in most boys. But then you add the sexual abuse, such as in my case and many, many boys like me. And then there is the peer labeling. A huge component is when you are labeled on campus as "fag" or "queer," and that label tends to be one that makes sense even though you hate it. It tends to be one that kind of defines you, and that can be incredibly solidifying in a person's identity even if you want to reject it with everything in you.

Question. This sexual abuse occurred from age eleven until eighteen. Tell us what happened when you went in to your high school counselor and confessed that you thought you might have same-sex attraction.

Mike. This was because of the shortcomings of the church. I didn't feel as though I could go and talk to anybody at church because, as I have said many, many times, the attitude from the pulpit of the church that I was raised in was that there was a hotter place than hell for gays and lesbians, or that Jesus had to hang a little longer on the cross for those people. And so church began to be uncomfortable. So I sought out a school counselor.

I went to see her because it was a safe haven, and I shared with her what was going on with me and what I was feeling. I didn't share the sexual abuse because I was smart enough to know that it would get this man in trouble, but it didn't feel abusive to me. This was a place where there was an older man paying attention to me, and that was something I needed. Sure, sex was a component, but what teenage boy isn't interested in sex? So I sat with her and shared with her what I was thinking, what I was feeling, that I didn't feel like one of the guys and that I was enjoying the sexual component of it all. Her response to me was that, from everything that she understood about the issue of homosexuality, you were born this way to live a healthy, productive life. From what I remember of the conversation, she said, "I know that you come from a religious family," and she encouraged me not to worry that my religious beliefs might be offended by the way I was living and that I should live true to who I am.

Question. So she was basically saying not to let your religious beliefs interfere with your feelings?

Mike. Right. Basically she was saying to live a healthy, productive life, you are going to have to rid yourself of the homophobia that you have learned religiously; to state it in narrow terms. This was again in the 1980s, so this has been going on for years and years. Thousands of students go to school counselors just as I did. Ask them to show you the resource list they use to help such students. You will be given completely pro-gay resources. You will never be told about NARTH—the National Association of Research and Therapy of Homosexuality—which is the most prolific organization of professionals that help men and women walk away from homosexuality from a clinical/psychological standpoint. You will never hear about Exodus International, which again is the largest Christian organization with hundreds of ministries worldwide that help men and women walk away from homosexuality and minister to the families as well. Help like this, which has helped thousands of people, is missing. Most counselors have never been told about it.

What impacted me so deeply was this counselor telling me I was born this way. It made sense to me when I was told there was a gay gene. That was the explanation for all of this—nature.

Question. Back up. You said "it made sense when I was told there was a gay gene."

Mike. Right. It made sense when I was told there was a gay gene, because it seemed I had always felt this way from as long as I can remember. I never chose to be gay. I only seemed to come to terms with it. And this news only confirmed it for me. But in a way it made me depressed for a while because I thought I really wanted a wife and kids. I wanted normalcy. But since I "had this gay gene," I thought, "well, this is who I am going to have to be the rest of my life." At that point I had pretty strong resolve as a person, and I think it worked against me. And I set my heart on the fact that I was going to be gay, and all there was now was to make the best of it.

Question. So you went full bore into living homosexually.

Mike. Absolutely. For the next twelve years, from the age of sixteen to twenty-eight, I was completely involved in the gay community. For a while I had my foot in the Christian community and lived a double life, and finally I just completely came out and pretty much left my faith behind. I wanted nothing more to do with Christianity for a number of years. I was living as a gay man, going from relationship to relationship. It was what all of my gay friends did.

Question. Melissa, your story is very different. How do you believe your same-sex attraction first developed?

Melissa. I have done a lot of thinking in my life and I have done a lot of research, and I have had to go back through the years of my childhood to see what the contributing factors were. What were the pieces, and how did they come together? The answer comes to five or six very significant things. I want to address a few of the most significant.

First, I really didn't form an emotionally connected relationship with my mother, and I think that left in my heart a lack of maternal love, a need for more of that motherly presence. My mother is and was somewhat emotionally reserved, stoic. I think I needed more affection as a young child, and I think that's how our personalities came together and left a deficit in my relationship with her. I think my dad—as I tried to look objectively at our relationship—was physically not in the home quite a bit due to other pressing demands that are normal as far as career and education and so forth. But I think that his lack of presence affected me, and I felt inadequate as a little girl.

Second is sexual abuse. The national estimates are 17 percent to 25 percent of all women are sexually abused. The conservative figure among women dealing with lesbianism is 60 percent. Personally, in my fifteen years of ministry in this area, I have not met a lesbian who had not been sexually abused or violated in some way. It was the same for me. So sexual abuse in my life created this fear and this distress and disdain toward men. I didn't see marriage as an institution or the roles of mother/wife modeled for me in a positive light. I did not want to be like my mother, and I did not want to have the life that she had because it looked very demanding and taxing, and it didn't seem that she was necessarily enjoying those roles.

Third, as Mike shared in his life, I too felt very inadequate in my gender, feeling very lacking when I compared myself with my peers. And it seemed as if they had all the pieces that it takes to be a girl, and I felt as if I were missing at least half, if not two-thirds of those pieces.

So those, I think, are the contributing factors as I have tried to look at my life in the past. So I think those pieces made me . . . I like to use the words *vulnerable* or *susceptible* to same-gender attractions or struggles. And it was really in my middle school years that I really began to recognize that I was not like the other girls. I was having crushes on the girls instead of crushes on the boys. I was very drawn emotionally to the girls and really began, I think, to put some pieces together that I must be gay.

Question. Looking back on that, what do you think you were really looking for in those other girls and women?

Melissa. What I was looking for in those other girls was—and I can say this is in adult language now—that motherly love, that nurture, that care, that tenderness, acceptance, affirmation from these other girls that I think was lacking in my relationship with my mother. I was looking for these other girls to fill this love deficit, this love need in my heart.

Question. How did that become sexualized for you?

Melissa. I can remember being drawn to girls emotionally as a young person in elementary school and then moving on to middle school, but certainly when puberty began to hit. I liken it to the picture that there were already fractures in the foundation, emotional fractures, and then when puberty hit those emotional fractures then became sexualized. And so at its core homosexuality, and lesbianism in particular, is about filling emotional, relational needs; that core need of wanting to connect with another girl but then, when entering into puberty, all of those feelings and emotions became sexualized.

[**Mike interrupts.** It would be good to ask Melissa, because she became very, very butch, why there was such a detachment from feminine things other than her lesbian life, much more than we see from the masculine in the gay male life.]

Question. Why do many lesbians actually start to take on almost a masculine look, a masculine persona, more so than homosexual men taking on a feminine persona?

Melissa. Certainly in my living as a lesbian for nearly a decade, it was my experience that a majority of the women had a very masculine look to them, and I call it "false masculine" now. In my own life I think there were several pieces there. From the home environment, the marriage that was modeled for me, I had a disdain for femininity, a disdain for womanhood, and so anything that represented femininity I abhorred. So I wanted to run away from it. And I think also because I had been sexually abused. For me, looking masculine and trying to come across as a man was in some ways my suit of armor, it was a sense of protection, to keep me safe from being violated again.

I had a lot of jealousy for boys and for men; their world seemed to be more appealing and more positive. Our society seems to affirm men more highly than women, and so in dressing masculine and having that false masculine exterior, it was feeding into that false masculine mentality inside of my mind. I was in some ways living out a fantasy of what I wished I could be but really wasn't. Not surprisingly, it never worked for me.

Question. There seems to be a real push-pull phenomenon with lesbians. You said you admired the masculine, but for many lesbians they really reject heterosexual males. And sometimes there is even an anger and a hatred toward the heterosexual male community.

Melissa. Often there's a very strong hatred of men among the lesbian community, and I think again that can be tied significantly to the reality of sexual abuse. For many of these women the abuse has gone underground in their hearts, if you will, and oftentimes that can erupt later on in life in an incredible rage. It was in the second year of my counseling that I finally understood why in the world I got drunk and punched concrete walls about every other night in college, which by the way, is not a smart thing to do. But I was doing this because of the abuse experience that I hadn't dealt with, and so this incredible rage. This sexual abuse manifests itself in a woman's life so she totally rejects men and then turns exclusively to women for love, affection and affirmation.

Question. Let's go back to an earlier point when you talked about your sexual abuse. How old were you when the sexual abuse occurred?

Melissa. I think it may be grace from the Lord that he hasn't allowed me to remember every piece of that sexual abuse. It is often protective that we block those horrible images out. What I can remember is that I was a young person, a little girl. I wasn't a teenager. It wasn't later on in those years but as a young girl. I knew that things had been done to me that were absolutely inappropriate, and they were of a sexual nature and they were at the hands of a male. I don't think it was in my home. I don't think it was someone in the family, and definitely was not my father or brother or anyone like that, but some male figure sometime in my life as a little girl.

Question. Mike and Melissa both of you know many gays and ex-gays; have you noticed similarities in their backgrounds?

Mike. Oh, absolutely. It's one of the things that surprised me often as I came to understand the roots of male homosexuality, and I was starting to learn those things during my time of involvement in the gay community. Back then, we'd be sitting at a house for Thanksgiving and there would be twelve to fifteen of my gay friends around, and we would begin to talk about our families. It was unbelievable to me how I began to see how none of my gay friends had relationships with their dads. They either disdained their fathers or were simply distant from them. And if they did have a positive relationship with them now as adult gay men, the years of their formation were incredibly tortured and there was an incredible strain there.

I looked at all of my gay male friends, and there was incredible familial trouble, strife, difficulty; there were no happy upbringings. Many of their parents were still together—it wasn't often divorce situations—but there was no "click" with the father. However, they all loved their moms; their moms were their best friends, and I just had to look at that and frankly laugh at how much the gay community fails to be honest about this. But on gay sitcoms like *Will & Grace* it's an inside running gag.

Question. Now let's come to the story of how each of you left. How were you able to stop living homosexually?

Melissa. I really like the words *progress* and *process*, and leaving homosexuality has certainly been multifaceted. So many people and so many events in my life were involved, but the most important part was that I eventually became a Christian. God touched me through real people. There were Christian men and women in my life who were overwhelming me with this unconditional love, this unconditional acceptance and grace. They knew that I was living homosexually, yet they were still so affirming and kind to me that I began to realize that I was at the proverbial end of my rope.

My life was miserable. I had lived homosexually for a decade, and it had reached its end. I was abusing alcohol almost daily and was beginning to get into drugs. I saw that I desperately needed a savior, and God revealed the grace of Jesus Christ and gave me that beautiful gift of salvation.

About a year before that time, though, God began to make me aware of my sin. I began to read Scripture, and very quickly realized that God certainly addresses this issue. Through his grace over about a year, he convinced me that he was right and that homosexuality indeed was wrong and was sin. Scripture teaches that repentance is a gift and that it's God's kindness that leads us to repentance, and so the Lord administered that repentance in my heart.

Scripture also teaches that we plan our course but that God orders our steps. And so in time God connected me with a ministry affiliated with Exodus International in the state where I was living, and I joined with that ministry and began counseling, support groups and reading dozens of books, attending conferences, beginning to learn how I became involved and what the contributing factors to homosexuality were. God began a very real restorative work in my mind. He began to bring all of these different pieces and people together along a time line that gradually, as a process, began to continue to bring me out of homosexuality.

I can say that what was most critical, crucial and significant is my relationship with the Lord, with the holy Trinity, the Father, the Holy Spirit and Jesus. That is what is paramount and will always be paramount, wanting to yield my life to my Lord, loving him because he first loved me, and wanting to model my life in agreement with his Scripture and with his empowering grace.

Question. Mike, how did you leave homosexuality?

Mike. My story is different. Mine was not due to a religious experience, although I was raised in the church and accepted the Lord from a very early age. I started looking toward the possibility of coming out of homosexuality because I got sick and tired of getting sick and tired. I got tired of the relationship failure. I looked around at all of my friends and none of them had long-term, monogamous relationships, although some of them had been able to stay together for a number of years. But the monogamy, real commitment, was just not there. As Melissa and I have often said, most people leave homosexuality holding the hand of a friend or a loved one, and for me that was the case. There was a man, Jeff Conrad, who wrote the book *You Don't Have to Be Gay*, which is one of the best resources for men that struggle and for any Christian who is interested in helping people in this area. Jeff lovingly, diligently and intentionally pursued me for five years, challenged my thinking, never intrusively but always in response to my questions. He'd send me things often, very thoughtful things: a birthday card that said "I love you. God loves you. Change is possible."

This man wouldn't give up on me. He lovingly and faithfully pursued me and patiently answered my questions and stood many times in the face of my intentional offense. When I would intentionally push him away with rudeness, he was just persistent. When I finally came to the end of myself, he was the first person I called. We are dear friends to this day.

Question. And you entered a residential treatment program. Can you briefly tell us about that?

Mike. Yeah, through Exodus International. Exodus has a number of different ways individuals can find help and support, whether it's a weekly drop-in group or whether it's a committed eighteen- to twenty-two-week group series that someone might go through, like the Living Waters Program. There are a couple of residential programs, and Living Waters is what I chose for myself.

I went to that, and it was unbelievable. I lived in a house with twelve other guys who were struggling with the same thing. A lot of people think, *How in the world did that work? It's like throwing alcoholics in a bar and telling them to quit drinking!* It's funny because when you live with these guys, their feet start to stink, their attitudes are abrasive, and you can't stand to be around them. Frankly, this is why homosexuality doesn't work anyway because when the mystique is gone and you are left with the other person sitting across the table from you, they are real, flawed and they are not what you want.

Question. How is that different than living with your wife?

Mike. They're worlds apart. When you are trying to find your whole essence in the other person, it is very different from heterosexual marriage. My wife constantly intrigues me; I am constantly trying to figure her out, and she is constantly trying to figure me out. We are constantly trying to come together, and there's intrigue, passion, but when it's male to male it loses that. You understand the masculine world, and you realize you are trying to fill yourself through the other individual, but it just doesn't work. And so living with these twelve other guys, as strange as that may sound to someone else, was incredibly healing for me because these men mirrored my life. When I saw them inappropriately, emotionally wanting to relate to a coworker they had, they would come back at night and talk about that because you live a normal life while you are there.

Question. How did it keep you accountable?

Mike. They would start to notice that on Friday nights I was like a caged animal. Part of that had to do with what I had been doing for the past twelve years. Friday nights had been getting ready, going to the gym, getting the perfect outfit on. [**Laughs.**] Listen to me. Heterosexual men don't wear "outfits." Going out to the bar to live my gay life. Friday night—when I was coming out of homosexuality—was like, "What do I do? This is not normal for me to sit."

I literally didn't know how to live, and that's much of why we need the church to be involved in this. We need people who understand. These guys would say to me, "Mike, you're like a caged animal!" They helped me understand what was going on for those twelve years and that there was behavior modification that needed to take place.

The gay community will often say to individuals like Melissa and me, "All you are really doing is just behavior modification." Frankly yes, there is some behavior modification. My behavior needed to change so I could allow those unmet, emotional needs that were being inappropriately met to rise to the top. I had to become uncomfortable enough with the old so that I would get them met appropriately. And that's where my healing began to come in and the sexual attraction began to fall away.

Question. We mentioned in this book that thousands of homosexuals have been able to change their sexual orientation. However, the research shows that many of them, while living productive heterosexual lives, still struggle with some residual same-sex attraction. How do each of you deal with that?

Mike. I deal with it by understanding where the attraction comes from, what the origination is and that it's wrong. Unhealthy attractions are there because of a specific reason. So once you understand those unmet emotional needs and have them fulfilled correctly, they tend to lose their power—once you understand where they are coming from. None of us are beyond anything that the world has to offer, whether it's alcoholism, homosexuality, adulterous affairs or even gossip. When we quit taking care of ourselves, quit being involved in strong accountability and living a disciplined Christian life, anytime we get away from that, the potential for us to buy into an inappropriate coping mechanism is there. Homosexual behavior and same-sex attractions are rooted in an inappropriate coping mechanism.

Melissa. When I began the journey out of homosexuality twelve years ago, I don't think I really thought about it at the time, but in retrospect I assumed that I would be married by now. So there are definitely several things I have had to look at and wrestle through in being in this journey.

I had to wrestle with the fact that maybe I had not arrived in the sense of femininity or womanhood, that there was still something wrong with me and the opposite gender didn't find me attractive, that I was not attractive enough to get a husband.

I had to wrestle with what people, even within the Exodus network, were thinking—that perhaps restoration hasn't happened in her life because she isn't married. I had to wrestle with the church. Oftentimes when I'm interviewed, the third or fourth question is "Are you married?" And I regret that question because when I say no, I feel like that answer in some way undermines the journey I have been on. But the opposite of lesbianism is not sex with a man but holiness toward God. The same goes for male homosexuality. That's the measuring stick.

At this point I've come to that peaceful place with the Lord that if he has done everything else in my life, then obviously in this season he has called me to singleness. Scripture teaches that marriage is a gift and singleness is a gift. I have had to lay the other things aside, what people think or what that says about my journey, and see that there are many benefits to being single: flexibility in travel and singular devotion to ministry. I treasure too, as the apostle Paul said, to have that singular devotion to Christ and not having my affections divided by a spouse and children, and I am resolved (and have peace in my heart) to stay single and serve the Lord in full-time ministry. It is truly a joy and an incredible privilege to be his handmaiden. But obviously too my heart has been radically changed with regard to men and marriage. And he could bring a man into my life this afternoon or tomorrow, and my heart would be fully opened to that reality. As Mike was sharing, I too had to learn that I probably would never find the entire male gender attractive, so it would have to be this one man who God brought into my life. It would be a falling in love with him because of who he is in Christ and being attracted to him in that relationship. But we will see; the last chapters have not been written yet.

Question. Can you speak to the man or woman who is struggling with same-sex attraction and offer them some hope?

Melissa. Yes. I can remember—even when I lived homosexually—I can remember commenting, "You know, if I could take a pill and I would wake up straight, I would take it in a heartbeat because there are so many challenges and heartaches involved with homosexuality." But at that time I could never fathom *not* being a lesbian. I had no reference point, no frame of mind to be any other way than gay or lesbian.

Now to look at my life and who I am (and of course I do because I live with myself 24/7, who else am I going to know!), knowing my mind, my heart, my decisions, hopes and dreams, and how I am different now from the person I was, I feel schizophrenic, to be honest. I don't even know who that person was compared to who I feel that I am now in Christ. So the reality of Christ on the cross and the empty tomb are the pinnacle reality of hope in any area of our lives that we are struggling with and want to overcome.

They are the pinnacle expression of hope that the Lord can do those miracles, and very specifically with regard to homosexuality and gender-identify confusion. How you engage and act with yourself and the opposite gender, all of those things can be changed. Absolutely, the hope that that can happen is because of Christ.

Mike. There are a couple of things that I would say. I think one is that there is hope for everyone, not just religiously minded Christians. There are ample amounts of research out that show change has taken place from a clinical/

psychological perspective since the 1930s. God does work in that also.

I praise God that I was able to do it through the strength of the Lord. I believe that the forgiveness goes far deeper, and the Lord has provided me the safe haven, the accountability of the church and the body of believers who surround me. But my life verse in giving hope to anybody is Hebrews 10:23, which says, "Let us hold unswervingly to the hope we profess, for he who promised is faithful."

You just have to make sure that your desire is God's desire, meaning that you may want marriage, a wife or husband and a picket fence, but that may not be what God has for you. So in falling in line and becoming obedient and living a life of holiness when your will becomes aligned with his is the best change you could possibly ever experience.

CHANGE IS POSSIBLE!

If you or a loved one is struggling with unwanted feelings of homosexuality, the following organizations can offer you wonderful help:

Focus on the Family's Love Won Out Conference and resources
<www.lovewonout.org>

Exodus International
<www.exodus-international.org>

NARTH (National Association for Research and Therapy of Homosexuality)
<www.narth.com>

Family Research Council
<www.frc.org>

Focus on the Family's *Focus on Social Issues*
<www.focusonsocialissues.org>

Index

abortion, 122-24

ACLU, 92

AIDS, 135, 142, 149

Akerlof, George, 96, 101

Amato, Paul R., 37, 70, 73

America's Women, 64, 96

American Academy of Pediatrics (AAP). *See* medical/mental health professional organizations

American Law Institute, 165

American Medical Association (AMA). *See* medical/mental health professional organizations

American Psychiatric Association (APA). *See* medical/mental health professional organizations

American Psychological Association. *See* medical/mental health professional organizations

Angel, Ronald J. and Jacqueline L., 37, 63, 70, 107

Anthony, Susan B., 35

anthropology, 47, 49

Bailey, Michael, 134, 136, 147

Baker v. Nelson, 38

Bancroft, John, 154

Barney & Friends, 68

Bayer, Ronald, 144-45

benefits, health care, 27-28

berdache, Native American, 51-52

Besen, Wayne, 150

Biblarz, Timothy, 72, 88, 106

Bieber, Irving, 136

Biller, Henry, 74, 75

Bing, Ellen, 37, 70, 74

Birch, Elizabeth, 133

Blankenhorn, David, 37, 55, 70

Boswell, John, 41-42

Bramlett, Matthew, 43

Buddhism, 40

Byne, William, 34, 135

C-250, Canadian bill, 42, 92

Campbell, Ethan, 154-55

Center for Law and Social Policy (CLASP), 104

Chambers, David, 164-65

child abuse, 72, 83-84, 91, 108

child development, 17, 37, 55-56, 70-75, 77, 78, 103, 119

Child Trends, 104

civil rights, 35-39, 42, 46, 137

civil unions, 42, 159

Clunis, Merilee, 71-72

Coates, Ta-Nehisi, 39

cohabitation, 30, 53, 55, 87, 96, 124-25

Collins, Gail. *See America's Women*

Coltrane, Scott, 37, 64, 70, 77, 91, 119

Conrad, Jeff, 186

constitutional right to marry, 32-33

contraception, 121-22

Coombs, Robert, 96, 98, 100

Council on Families in America, 44

Dahomey, women "marriage" in, 50-51

Dawson, Deborah, 37, 63, 70, 105, 107

deconstruction, family/humanity, 61, 157, 163, 174

of gender, 56-58, 124

"Defining Deviancy Down," 65

de Silva, Alvaro, 7

Diagnostic and Statistical Manual of Mental Disorders, The (DSM), 144-45

discrimination, 42, 92, 149

divorce, 30, 44-46, 53, 55, 68-69, 82, 85-89, 97-100, 104-5, 107, 123, 185

effects on children, 37, 44, 85-87

Glenn T. Stanton is director of social research and cultural affairs, and senior analyst for marriage and sexuality, at Focus on the Family.

He is the author of *Why Marriage Matters* (Piñon/NavPress, 1997) and a contributor to many books, including *Same-Sex Marriage: The Moral and Legal Debate* (Prometheus Books, 2004). His book *My Crazy, Imperfect Christian Family* (NavPress, 2004) explores the virtue of imperfect families and the sacredness of the mundaneness of family life.

Stanton has published articles in *Christianity Today*, the *American Enterprise*, *Family Policy*, *National Forum*, *Dr. Laura's Perspective* and others. He is also a winner of the 2001 Amy Foundation Writing Award and featured in the PBS documentary *Affluenza*. As a media spokesperson for Focus on the Family, he has been interviewed by hundreds of print and media outlets, including MSNBC and CNN, and quoted in the *New York Times*, the *Washington Post*, *USA TODAY*, *Salon.com*, *Newsweek*, *Rolling Stone*, the *Washington Blade* and the *Advocate*.

A graduate of the University of West Florida, Stanton earned a master's degree in interdisciplinary humanities with an emphasis in philosophy, history and religion. He has taught in each of these disciplines.

Stanton and his wife have five children and make their home in Colorado Springs, Colorado.

Dr. Bill Maier is a clinical psychologist and serves as vice-president and psychologist in residence at Focus on the Family.

He hosts the national *Weekend Magazine* radio program and *The Family Minute with Dr. Bill Maier*. He is a regular contributor to *Focus on the Family* magazine and has written for *Current Thoughts and Trends*, *Today's Christian Woman*, the *Houston Chronicle* and the *Colorado Springs Gazette*.

Dr. Maier received his master's and doctoral degrees from the Rosemead School of Psychology at Biola University. He has served at respected institutions such as Childrens Hospital Los Angeles, Camarillo State Hospital and the Long Beach Child Guidance Center. He has extensive experience in parent training and education, and his major area of research interest is the impact of cultural trends on child development and family functioning.

The Maier family lives in Colorado Springs, Colorado.